Women Making a Difference in Marriage

Building Love, Joy, and Commitment

Lana Packer

LifeWay Press
Nashville, Tennessee

ISBN: 07673-93775

This book is a resource in the Home/Family category of the Christian Growth Study Plan. Course CG-0655

Dewey Decimal Classification Number: 306.81
Subject Heading: MARRIAGE \ WOMEN \ WIVES

Photograher: Michael W. Rutherford

Unless otherwise indicated, all Scripture quotations are from the Holy Bible, *New International Version*, copyright © 1973, 1978, 1984 by International Bible Society. Used by permission.
Scripture quotations identified NKJV are from the *New King James Version*. Copyright © 1979, 1980, 1982, Thomas Nelson, Inc. Publishers. Used by permission. Verses marked TLB are taken from *The Living Bible*.
Copyright © Tyndale House Publishers, Wheaton, Illinois, 1971. Used by permission.
Scripture quotations identified AMP are taken from *The Amplified New Testament*
© The Lockman Foundation 1954, 1958, 1987. Used by permission.
Scripture taken from the NEW AMERICAN STANDARD BIBLE (NASB),
© Copyright The Lockman Foundation, 1960, 1962, 1963, 1968, 1971, 1972, 1973, 1975, 1977, 1995 Used by permission.
Scripture quotations identified RSV are taken from the *Revised Standard Version of the Bible*, copyrighted 1946, 1952, © 1971, 1973.
Scripture marked Phillips is reprinted with permission of Macmillan Publishing Co., Inc. from J.B. Phillips: *The New Testament in Modern English*, Revised Edition. © J.B. Phillips 1958, 1960, 1972.
Scripture quotations identified KJV are from the *King James Version*.

To order additional copies of this resource: WRITE LifeWay Church Resources Customer Service; One LifeWay Plaza; Nashville, TN 37234-0113; FAX order to (615) 251-5933; PHONE (800) 458-2772; EMAIL to *customerservice@lifeway.com*; ORDER ONLINE at *www.lifeway.com*; or VISIT the LifeWay Christian Store serving you.

Printed in the United States of America

✠

Adult Ministry Publishing
LifeWay Church Resources
One LifeWay Plaza
Nashville, TN 37234-0175

Table of Contents

About the Author

Lana Packer is a Women's Ministry Bible Study leader for International Baptist Church in Singapore, where her husband David is pastor. Lana is a gifted Bible teacher and caring counselor. She has a Bachelor of Science degree from Texas Women's University School of Nursing in Dallas, Texas.

Lana and David were Southern Baptist missionaries to the Philippines for eight years. They returned to the United States to begin a new church in South Texas and then were called to the church in Singapore, where thirty-five nationalities gather each Sunday for worship.

Lana enjoys traveling throughout the world and has been on several mission trips sponsored by her church. She enjoys entertaining, shopping, and sampling different cuisine. The Packers have three adult children, Jonathan, Matthew, and Amy.

Women Making a Difference in Marriage is based on a study which Lana has taught in many settings and cultures throughout the world.

About the Study

Women Making a Difference in Marriage is an 8-week study in the Women's Enrichment Resources® series. This unique study is written to women, not couples, and is designed to be discussed in a small group by women who want to honor God in their marriage relationships.

The study is an interactive Bible study with five daily lessons each week. The daily lessons, to be completed on your own, should take no more than 20 minutes each. The learning activities help you apply what you learn to your personal situation. They also encourage you to go to God's Word for answers to everyday situations.

Following each week of individual study, you will gather with other women for small-group discussions that will give you opportunity to learn from others' marital experiences. A leader guide is provided on pages 181-191.

If you have not made the important and life-changing decision to accept Jesus Christ as your personal Lord and Savior, turn to page 25 for information on how to become a Christian.

Introduction

As a teenager, I wondered what it would be like to be in love. In my youthful dreams, my wedding day would be perfect. Wearing a flowing gown, I would walk down the aisle in a garden full of flowers with violin music playing in the background. Then on the arm of my handsome groom, we would exit the garden with everyone admiring this wonderful couple. As I looked toward the future, I knew that when I found that perfect man, I would live in joy and happiness from that point forward.

Then I met my true love! He was the handsome man of my dreams, and he was preparing to be a minister—so I knew he must be perfect. I was the most blessed of women! After the wedding, we drove off into the sunset, not on a white horse but in a white Volkswagen. Unfortunately, my brothers had decorated our car in a most unbecoming way. My new husband was furious! *Well, maybe he isn't perfect*, I thought. We were just beginning our honeymoon, and a little bit of reality came creeping in.

We each come into marriage with preconceived ideas of what we need and want. A necessary part of growing in our marriages is understanding and accepting that many of these expectations are unattainable. Today, the world tells us that everyone deserves to be happy, and we are to do whatever it takes to get our portion of what the world has to offer. Our life mission is then to find the happiness and joy that we expect. We look to people or circumstances and then possessions to fill the void that constantly seems to be with us. For many women marriage is supposed to fill this ever-present void. Yet the divorce rate, even among Christians, shows that joy and contentment are not found consistently in marriage.

Others look to marriage as a new beginning—a place where they can leave past failures and hurts behind. Hopes soar high on their wedding day as they enter this new realm of existence. Within the first few weeks of marriage, they realize that they are the same people they were on their wedding day, and they are not sure they even like the person they married. The old problems enter into the new relationship.

One thing is for certain: we will experience problems in marriage! No matter whom we marry or how well we are matched, difficulties and differences arise. So what are we to do? How can we live a life of joy when we have little control over the people, circumstances, or trials that come our way? We must first understand that God has a plan for our marriages. God wants to remold our dreams and conform them to His purposes for our lives.

During this study, we will examine God's plan and affirm His vision for our marriages. Then we can begin building, or sometimes re-building, our marriages according to His design. If we look to our husbands or to our marriages as the source of lasting joy, we will be disappointed. The only place where joy is found is in Jesus Christ! Jesus can fill all of our needs for love, unconditional acceptance, and lasting joy. If we look to other people, joy will never be consistent. This study will focus on the One and only true Source to meet the needs of our hearts, instead of focusing on temporary fixes for our marriages.

Although marriage is not to be the ultimate source of our joy and fulfillment, God designed marriage to be a wonderful life-long love affair. God is the Creator of marriage and the Author of love. Through carefully studying the Bible and adopting a willingness to follow its principles, instructions, and examples, we can begin to experience all that God intended for our marriages. Because God conceived the idea of marriage and ordained it, He also provides His resources to build love, joy, and commitment in our marriages. As we apply His principles, we can restore the newness and sweetness we felt on our wedding day.

God works His miracles to change hearts, one heart at a time. Even if your spouse is not cooperating with God's plan, He can still richly bless you and your family. God can enable you to be the spouse you should be even if you have a rebellious spouse. This study has something for every situation. I have taught this study to several cultures in different countries. The women you will meet are real, although their names have been changed. I have seen the Lord's miracles in countless marriages that seemed hopeless. I have seen other marriages revived and energized. Yes, ladies, you can make a difference in your marriage!

In this study you will read about my husband David and our three children—Jonathan, Matthew, and Amy—who are now young adults. You will follow our family from the United States to the Philippines, back again to the States, then to Singapore where we now reside. I hope our family's struggles, twists, and turns will encourage you and give you hope. However, this study is not about the Packers.

This study is about you and what God has for you. It is about finding the joy that the Lord offers you in abundance in your personal life and in your marriage! Will you take a moment right now and commit your marriage to the Lord? Ask Him to help you give all your plans and hopes to Him. God is faithful and will bless you in ways you never could have imagined. In the space at the top of the page, write your personal expectations for this study. What needs led you to this study? What hopes and dreams do you have for your marriage?

_____

_____

_____

Then write a prayer asking God to make you moldable. Be specific and be honest. God knows your heart. You will not be asked to share this prayer with your group.

Dear God, _____

_____

_____

As you start this journey, I pray that God will become even more real to you and be magnified in your life. I am also praying for the time you and your group will spend together. My prayer is that you will grow together in fellowship as you grow closer to the Lord and as your marriages grow stronger.

In His lavish love,

Lana Packer

Lana Packer
Singapore

Lasting Joy

This week you will learn that

- your significance comes from God, not others;
- your role is an exalted position that comes from strength, not weakness;
- a suitable helper protects her husband's heart and provides companionship;
- sin has distorted all of our love relationships;
- Christ is the source of lasting joy—a joy that can be lived out in your marriage.

Did you know that you can rent wedding rings? If your marriage fails, you don't lose your investment. Many couples begin marriage without a sense of commitment. Unfortunately, the divorce rate among Christians is about the same as the general public. If marriage is supposed to bring happiness, why do so many marriages fail?

Often, we equate happiness—that temporary euphoria that comes from what is going on around us—with joy. Lasting joy that comes from God does not depend on circumstances, possessions, or people. Happiness can never replace deep and abiding joy.

Perhaps you feel God's joy in your life and marriage right now. You may be studying this topic as a way of continuing to build a solid faith-based marriage as an enduring legacy to all who know you.

Perhaps you believe that joy is not possible for you because your husband is not a believer or he is out of step with God's will for his life. Perhaps you feel the two of you are mismatched or that you are carrying too much baggage in your marriage.

Let me assure you that God's joy is available no matter what your circumstances or whom you married. Even during difficult times, He promises His living presence and power. Even when we fail, God promises never to leave or forsake us (Josh. 1:5).

Is it ever too late to experience joy? No. How does God work? Through the presence of the Holy Spirit, God changes our hearts, attitudes, and, ultimately, our behavior. We must never forget that we have the divinely inspired handbook on marriage—the Word of God!

Let me encourage you about the future of your marriage. The relationship you would like to have can happen! This relationship won't just happen by chance or by positive thinking but by applying what God says in His Word. Change will occur!

In our study this week we will examine the first chapters of the Bible. Our marriages are so important to God that He started at the very beginning giving us principles to guide us. These basic principles are the foundation we will build on for the remainder of this study.

Day 1

Uniquely Designed

God created man in his own image, in the image of God he created him; male and female he created them. Genesis 1:27

Each of my children was born with unique features and personalities, but no one can deny that they are my children. As a new mother, I spent hours examining my first born—his beautiful face, every finger, and all 10 little toes. Words really cannot describe the awesome feeling of those moments. Each part perfect and intricate! Jonathan's coloring was definitely the same skin tone as my husband's, but his eyes were mine.

When my second child was born, Matthew looked so much like David that it was almost unbelievable. Everyone said he was a carbon copy of his father. In effect, he was the image of his father.

We are made in God's image.

In Genesis 1:24-27, human life was created differently than animal

life. How were the living creatures made? _____

_____

In whose image were they made? _____

In whose image was man (male and female) made? _____

The animals were created according to their kinds, but mankind was created in God's image. When God finished creating the animals, He saw that "it was good" (v. 25), but when God finished creating mankind, He saw that "it was very good" (v. 31).

God said, "Let the land produce living creatures according to their kinds: livestock, creatures that move along the ground, and wild animals, each according to it's kind." And it was so. God made the wild animals according to their kinds, and all the creatures that move along the ground according to their kinds. And God saw that it was good.

Then God said, "Let us make man in our image, in our likeness, and let them rule over the fish of the sea and the birds of the air, over the livestock, over all the earth, and over all the creatures that move along the ground."

So God created man in his own image, in the image of God he created him; male and female he created them. Genesis 1:24-27

9

The fact that we are made in God's image shows us the unique value we have in His eyes. God's creation of you and me was according to His plans and purposes, and He made no mistakes! Notice that we were created in the image of the Trinity: God the Father, God the Son, and God the Spirit. All three Persons of the Godhead were present.

Believing and accepting that we are uniquely designed by God can have a profound impact on the way we view ourselves. Katie (not her real name) was a beautiful young teenager in our church. People were attracted to her, not just because of her physical beauty—even though she was very pretty—but also because of her inner beauty. She had a grace that exuded confidence, and she was kind to everyone.

In school, Katie excelled in both academics and extracurricular activities. She won almost every award the school offered. She always seemed to be surrounded by friends, both boys and girls. In her final year of high school, she won the school's beauty contest.

When I congratulated her, she replied, "I just don't understand. I'm not pretty at all!" After spending time talking with her, I realized that she really felt very ugly. In her opinion, many others were much prettier. As her story unfolded, I learned that as a child, the muscles around her eyes were very weak, and as a result, she was cross-eyed. Others would make fun of her, imitating how she looked, and once someone said, "Only someone dumb would look like you do."

That child's thoughtless statement never completely left Katie's thoughts. Finally, after much heartache, her parents scheduled a surgery to correct her eyes. The surgery was not a success and left her eyes over-corrected or walleyed. After several more surgeries, her eyes were corrected, but her self-image did not fully recover. Those images of herself as a child influenced the way she thought about herself. She never felt worthy of total acceptance from others.

We each have hurts from the past that have shaped how we feel about ourselves. Some of these feelings come from our families, and others occur from external events. We carry these feelings of doubt and low self-esteem into our marriages. Often we expect our husbands to meet our need for acceptance, yet God never intended that another person would meet the needs that only He can meet. Whatever the source of our feelings of self-doubt, God has a remedy: accepting the unique value we have in His sight.

Know that God created you the way you are, and He is incapable of making a mistake. When you accept the truth that you are created in

God never intended that another person would meet the needs that only He can meet.

God's image and that He loves you unconditionally, you can begin to see yourself as loved and precious in His sight. Out of His abundant love, we are able to love others as ourselves (Mark 12:31).

One of the greatest gifts you can give your husband is developing a healthy self-image. When you free him from having to be your source of self-esteem, he will feel an enormous weight lifted from his shoulders. It is a weight God never intended him to carry.

 Have you burdened your husband with being the source of your self-esteem? (circle)   yes   no
If so, will you free him today of that burden? (circle)   yes   no

Find a time and a quiet place to ask your husband's forgiveness. Tell him that you want to find your acceptance in God. Ask for and thank him for his support as you seek to live out this truth.

We are to be like God.

We are made in God's image, not only intellectually and emotionally but also spiritually. We can respond to His Spirit's voice. We can communicate with God. Isn't that exciting? No matter what the circumstances, we have the Spirit of God within us helping us and guiding us. Not only are we created in God's image, but we are created to be like God.

 In Ephesians 4:22-24 underline how we are to be like God.

In Ephesians 2:10 underline what were we created to do.

Paul encouraged the new believers in Ephesus to pursue lives of righteousness and holiness, always doing good works as they accepted the responsibility of being heirs of God. Because we are made in God's image, we have the responsibility to live like His children and show God's image to the world through our lives.

One way we reflect God's image is found in Genesis 1: 28. Like our Creator God, the Source of all life, we are to "be fruitful and multiply" (NKJV). I believe this command can validly be applied in the spiritual realm to multiplying our faith in others. When we find our significance in God, we have a powerful message to the world around us. Often that message is first shared with our own families (see Mal. 2:15), but it should be spread beyond the walls of our homes and churches.

You were taught, with regard to your former way of life, to put off your old self, which is being corrupted by its deceitful desires; to be made new in the attitude of your minds; and to put on the new self, created to be like God in true righteousness and holiness.
Ephesians 4:22-24

We are God's workmanship, created in Christ Jesus to do good works, which God prepared in advance for us to do.
Ephesians 2:10

Tell about the person who first introduced you to God. How did he

or she reflect God's image? _____

_____

_____

After God created Adam and Eve, He saw that "it was very good" (Gen. 1:31). God created men and women different from the animals, even different from one another, as coheirs in His kingdom.

At the beginning of creation God "made them male and female."
Mark 10:6

Underline what Jesus said about our creation in Mark 10:6?

God could have created only men or only women, but He chose to create men and women. Wouldn't it have been a boring world if there were only one gender? Not only did God create two distinct genders, but He also gave them corulership over the animals and the world He made. Nowhere in the Bible does God withdraw this responsibility. God created you and has a plan for your life. Because you are married, His plan includes your marriage. You will find it difficult to have a joy-filled marriage if you are not a joy-filled person. Joy comes from the inside out. Joy begins with knowing who you are.

Today's lesson is very basic, but it is the foundation for understanding God's plan for your marriage. Knowing that you are so highly valued by God can have a profound impact on you and, in turn, your spouse. Will you write a prayer thanking God for creating you, not as an afterthought, but as an intentional act? If you are not thankful for the way you were created, will you honestly tell God that and ask Him to help you to be thankful for every aspect of yourself?

Dear God, _____

_____

_____

Day 2

An Exalted Position

The Lord God said, "It is not good for the man to be alone. I will make a helper suitable for him." Genesis 2:18

Growing up as the oldest of five children, I was used to giving orders. Often I resented being the oldest, as I had to baby-sit for my younger siblings, but at other times I enjoyed the position of authority that my birth order gave me. When I got married, the rules changed. No longer did I have the authority to tell my husband what to do; in fact, he was telling me things I should do.

We both were searching for a position of power, and it brought us to a point of decision. Either we could each seek to assert our own rights, or we could seek God and His truth on the issues we faced. The key to my relinquishing control came from my study of the role of the wife in a godly marriage. Today, we will examine this role based on God's Word.

Let's be honest with each other. How do you feel about being described as your husband's helper? In most cultures, the word *helper* refers to someone who assists a person of greater status or worth. In Genesis 2:18, God did not paint this picture at all. In fact, the word *helper* is an exalted word in Scripture.

God is our helper.

In day 1 you learned that God created you uniquely and gave you great value. He made no mistakes. In Genesis 1:31, God saw that all of His creation was "very good."

Read Genesis 2:18. What was not good? _____

What was God's solution to man's aloneness? _____

The Lord God said, "It is not good for the man to be alone. I will make a helper suitable for him." Genesis 2:18

God, the Creator, saw that man, His creature, was alone, and He announced that it definitely, without a doubt, was NOT GOOD! God saw a need and then provided a wonderful and creative solution. "I will make a helper suitable for him" (v. 18). The man was perfectly made in a perfect environment but not complete. He needed help.

What do you think of when you hear the word *helper?*

_____

Surely God is my help;
the Lord is the one who
sustains me.
Psalm 54:4

How does David describe God in Psalm 54:4? _____

Oh ladies, let us never forget that God is our personal Helper. Just like David in Psalm 30:10, we can cry out to God, "be my help." Is God less than us because He is our ever-present Helper in all situations? Of course not! God helps us from a position of strength and power.

We say with confidence,
"The Lord is my helper;
I will not be afraid.
What can man do
to me?"
Hebrews 13:6

Why is it such a comfort that God is our helper (Heb. 13:6)?

_____

_____

God often refers to Himself as the helper of His people. Jesus said that He came to serve and not to be served (Matt. 20:28), and the ideal Christian attitude toward others is the attitude of a helper. The one who gives receives more than he gives (Acts 20:36). One of the gifts of the Spirit is the gift of helps (1 Cor. 12:28). Make no mistake: to be a helper is an exalted position from God's perspective.

Man had a need.

A cultural value in many places around the world suggests that a real man needs no help. He is self-sufficient and can take care of himself quite well. He is always in control and never at a loss for what to do. Some cultures say that it is actually the woman who needs help. She is the weak and vulnerable partner who has many needs.

Husbands, in the same way
be considerate as you live
with your wives, and treat
them with respect as the
weaker partner and as heirs
with you of the gracious gift
of life, so that nothing will
hinder your prayers.
1 Peter 3:7

Doesn't 1 Peter 3:7 support this conclusion? Tell how the woman is

described: _____

In Greek the weaker partner, or vessel, referred to a cherished piece of pottery (like china) of great value—something to be cherished above all else. Peter said that if a husband did not recognize and treat his wife as an heir of God's grace, his prayers would be hindered.

Scripture clearly states that it was not the woman who was in need of a helper; indeed, the man was in need of help.

Read Genesis 2:19-20. After God identified Adam's need, He gave Adam a task. Underline it.

Interestingly, God paraded before Adam all the animals, and Adam named them. Picture this scene for a moment. God had just identified a need in Adam's life, and He also proposed a solution; then He asked Adam to name the animals! I imagine God smiled as Adam searched for that very special "helper" He had designed just for him. Adam probably thought, *No, that elephant couldn't be the one, it's too big.* Or, *That giraffe couldn't be it, for the neck is much too long for my liking!*

I believe God was giving Adam time so he would understand his great need for a companion. He saw that all the animals had a perfect partner, and he knew that his partner could not come from the animals. He trusted God as the only One who could create someone who would perfectly correspond to his needs.

God provided the solution.

In Genesis 2:21-22, God created the woman. What a fabulous scene! God caused Adam to sleep and then He fashioned out of Adam's rib a specific woman for Adam. The word *fashion* indicates taking care to build, to mold into something beautiful for a specific need. God brought the rib to life. Eve was the lovely creature, that "suitable helper" that God envisioned for Adam. In the book *Love Life for Every Married Couple* the authors describe beautifully what this helper is to do:

"We have often heard it said that God did not take Eve from Adam's head so that she would rule over him, or from his feet so that she would be his slave. There is some real truth in this. But what kind of picture is God giving to us by taking Eve from Adam's rib? Our ribs protect our most vital organs. Our ribs protect our heart. This would be one of Eve's ministries in the life of her husband—she would give protection to his heart!"[1]

The Lord God had formed out of the ground all the beasts of the field and all the birds of the air. He brought them to the man to see what he would name them; and whatever the man called each living creature, that was its name. So the man gave names to all the livestock, the birds of the air and all the beasts of the field.

But for Adam no suitable helper was found.
Genesis 2:19-20

In the early years of our marriage when David and I were defining what it meant to be a couple, we would often entertain couple friends. I still remember cringing when a wife began describing her husband both in his presence and out of his presence as unsuccessful and sexually inadequate. I have thought back to those words many times and have literally groaned for this husband. Although we can agree on the inappropriateness of these comments, we must examine our own words to and about our husbands. I can remember times I have had to apologize to my husband for words that exposed and wounded him.

 Examine your words now. Do your words protect your husband's heart or pull him down? Describe a time when your words have not protected your husband's heart.

_____

_____

Do you need to ask for your husband's forgiveness for some words you have spoken? If so, plan a time when you can apologize.

Recall that God addressed Adam's aloneness by creating Eve. We are to provide our husbands with companionship. We are to be recreational companions as well as physical, emotional, and spiritual companions.

In his book *His Needs, Her Needs*, Willard F. Harley, Jr., identified five needs each of husbands and wives from his years of counseling experience. The number two need expressed by husbands was for wives to be recreational companions.[2]

Which of your husband's interests or hobbies do you share? Are you willing to spend time in ways that may entertain him more than you? Of course, in the ideal give-and-take of a healthy relationship, both husband and wife would willingly give time and energy to the other spouse's interests. However, we cannot withhold our companionship while waiting for the ideal relationship. If necessary, set a sacrificial example in obedience to God's calling on your life.

 What will you do this week to be a companion to your husband?

_____

Day 3
A Suitable Helper

The Lord God made a woman from the rib he had taken out of the man, and he brought her to the man. Genesis 2:22

God created us in His image and then commissioned men and women to rule over the earth and the animals. They were to "be fruitful and increase in number" (Gen. 1:28). Neither the man nor the woman could perform this function alone.

In fact, Adam's aloneness was the reason given for Eve's creation. Adam couldn't have a personal relationship with the animals. Adam needed a helper, and God fashioned one who would be ideal for him. When considering the wife's role, we must remind ourselves that God made the first couple just exactly the way He planned. No mistakes were made. God called His creation good; in fact, it was very good!

Wives are intended to act as godly counterparts to our husbands because our natures supply what is lacking in theirs. A suitable helper is a completer and a complementer to her husband. Her motivation behind loving actions is the desire to meet the deep inner needs of her husband. This process doesn't happen overnight; it is a lifetime commitment.

A suitable helper understands her identity.

In day 2, we learned that a suitable helper is an exalted title often used to describe God. God did not create us as second-class individuals. We are "heirs ... of the gracious gift" (1 Pet. 3:7). When you realize that your true worth and significance come only from God, then you are free to love your husband despite what he may do or say.

> Your true worth and significance come only from God.

A lady in one of my marriage classes confided that her husband was living with another woman. Even though the situation seemed hopeless, she remained committed to their marriage. She related that at times her husband's words and actions made her feel worthless. She had always taken pride in being his wife, and making a home for him was her full-time career. Suddenly, her world had been shattered.

When she felt like she was just hanging on by a thread with her husband standing over her with scissors, she focused on her value to God. He gave her significance no matter what her husband or the world thought. This realization pulled her through some difficult times.

Oh ladies, I can't say it enough. Don't allow your husband to be the source of your identity. You have unconditional love from your Father who values you as His child. Claim your identity in Him. Take time to focus on who God is and what He has done for you instead of focusing on what your husband is doing or not doing.

Check the statements that are true for you.

- [ ] I often allow my husband's opinion of me to carry more weight than God's opinion.
- [ ] I value myself because I am God's creation.
- [ ] I can accept my role as helper as an exalted position.

A suitable helper loves and obeys God.

As wives, we will never be able to love our husbands the way we should if we do not love the Lord our God with all our hearts, souls, minds, and strength (Mark 12:30). Recall that the first two of the Ten Commandments tell us to worship no other gods. Is it possible for a husband to be an idol?

Perhaps you may feel that worshipping your husband is the least of your worries! However, when you give him priority in terms of your thoughts, feelings, and actions, you have made him an idol—even if you are in a less-than-satisfying relationship. Actually, we are more prone to obsess about our husbands when things are not going well. If you have been guilty of putting your husband ahead of God, confess that sin to Him today.

We are faced with the choice of obedience. Will we obey all that God has commanded us to do as wives? Will we obey God even when our husbands treat us unfairly? Obedience has never been easy, but with it comes a deeper love relationship with God as we learn to trust Him and realize that our significance and inheritance come only from Him!

Check the statements that are true for you.

- [ ] I find myself focusing on my husband rather than on God.
- [ ] My relationship with God seems to go up or down depending on my relationship with my husband.
- [ ] I have made my husband an idol in my life.
- [ ] My husband knows that God is in first place in my life.
- [ ] Pleasing God will always have the greatest importance as I make daily choices.

Is it possible for a husband to be an idol?

A suitable helper nurtures her marriage.

Although our husbands are not to be our priority relationship, they are to be our primary earthly relationship. Study after study shows that loneliness is a major marital problem. You may reside in the same house, have sex together, and share a checking account, but without love or communication, you may still feel you live alone. Unless you actively nurture your marriage, you will begin to drift away from your husband.

Is your husband truly the most important relationship you have? I have talked to many husbands who relate that they want no more children because they feel they already compete with their children for attention from their wives. Some men are jealous of their wives' jobs because they feel they are second in line, not only in time but in commitment. Other husbands have expressed anger against the church because their wives seem more committed to the church than to them.

We show our husbands that they are our primary earthly relationship by deferring to them above all other people, including our children or parents. In order for the new relationship between bride and groom to flourish and their home to begin correctly, the cord must be cut with the parents. This action does not mean abandoning our parents or ignoring, mistreating, or cutting off all contact with them. To "leave his father and mother" means to break the parent-child bond, to sever the tight, emotionally dependent strings that once provided security, protection, financial assistance, and the meeting of physical needs (Gen. 2:24).

 List one thing that you can do to show your husband that your relationship with him is the most important earthly one you have.

Has your view concerning being a helper to your husband changed during your study this week? If so, how? Ask the Lord to give you the heart of a godly suitable helper. Be honest; He knows your heart. Then ask the Lord to show you practical ways you can begin to help your husband—not just physically but emotionally as well.

Has God spoken to you this week about the way you think about your husband, your circumstances, or the people around you? How do you need to think differently? Thoughts precede actions. If we are going to act lovingly toward our husbands, we need to begin by thinking of them in loving ways.

In I Corinthians 13 Paul describes love as actions. In the following list, underline the words that best describe love according to I Corinthians 13: 4-7.

patient   unforgiving   kind   envious
protective   rejoicing in truth   boastful   hopeless
angry   trusting   rude   persevering

A suitable helper stands on God's Word.

In order for us to demonstrate the love of I Corinthians 13, our priority relationship must be with God. Then we must depend on His indwelling Spirit to produce the fruit of the Spirit (Gal. 5: 22-23). We cannot show God's love unless we know Him personally and allow His Spirit full access to our thoughts, words, and actions.

One of the outgrowths of a dynamic personal relationship with God is a love for His Word, the Bible. A suitable helper knows the Word of God. To be more specific, she must know what the Word of God has to say about marriage. You have taken an important step by enrolling in this study. Expect Satan to oppose you. He doesn't want you to know or live out God's design for your marriage. Let me encourage you to be diligent and to continue, for God will truly bless, and you will experience that deep abiding peace and joy that comes only from the Lord!

A Suitable Helper

1. Understands her identity.
2. Loves and obeys God.
3. Nurtures her marriage.
4. Stands on God's word.

 As we close today's lesson, ask God to give you His love for your husband. God wants to love your husband through you. Tell God that you are willing to show love to your husband for His sake, rather than basing your love on your husband's words or actions.

Dear God, _____

_____

_____

Day 4

Affected by the Fall

The eyes of both of them were opened, and they realized they were naked; so they sewed fig leaves together and made coverings for themselves. Genesis 3:7

God created a wonderful world—beautiful and harmonious. He designed the relationship between a man and woman to be completely fulfilling and satisfying. However, when we look at our world today, instead of companionship in marriage, we see misunderstanding and resentment. Instead of cooperation, we see conflict. Instead of compassion, we see abuse—both physical and emotional. Why isn't marriage the way God designed it? What went wrong?

In the third chapter of Genesis we encounter a sinister being whose actions and intentions dramatically oppose those of Creator God. From the beginning Satan's entire purpose has been to deceive and destroy. He used the first married couple to introduce sin into the world, and the marriage relationship has not been the same since.

Deceived by Satan

 Read Genesis 3:1. Underline Satan's question.

Satan appeared in disguise as a serpent and posed his first question: " 'Did God really say, "You must not eat from any tree in the garden" '?" Satan focused on what Adam and Eve could not do instead of all that God had done for them. Isn't that the way we often view life? We look at the prohibitions instead of all the good things God has provided.

Eve stated that they couldn't eat the fruit or even touch it because God said they would surely die (Gen. 3:3). The serpent immediately retorted, "You will not surely die." He cast doubt on the truth of God's Word. The serpent's next tactic was to make Eve doubt God's good character: "For God knows that when you eat of it your eyes will be opened, and you will be like God, knowing good and evil" (Gen. 3:5).

Satan boldly uses these two tactics today! We don't believe God's Word, so we disobey His commands. We doubt His goodness and question His love for us, so we try to take care of ourselves in our own way.

The serpent was more crafty than any of the wild animals the Lord God had made. He said to the woman, "Did God really say, 'You must not eat from any tree in the garden'?" Genesis 3:1

Adam was not the one deceived; it was the woman who was deceived and became a sinner.
1 Timothy 2:14

The eyes of both of them were opened, and they realized they were naked; so they sewed fig leaves together and made coverings for themselves.
Genesis 3:7

The Lord God called to the man, "Where are you?"
He answered, "I heard you in the garden, and I was afraid because I was naked; so I hid."
And he said, "Who told you that you were naked? Have you eaten from the tree that I commanded you not to eat from?"
The man said, "The woman you put here with me—she gave me some fruit from the tree, and I ate it."
Genesis 3:9-12

Then the Lord God said to the woman, "What is this you have done?" The woman said, "The serpent deceived me, and I ate."
Genesis 3:13

Eve saw the fruit, concluded that she needed it, and then gave it to her husband who was with her. I wonder why Adam didn't interrupt the process. Why didn't he say, "No, we shouldn't do this"? First Timothy provides insight into Eve's actions.

Read I Timothy 2:14. Why did Eve sin? _____

The Scripture is careful not to put all the blame on Eve. It says, instead, that she was thoroughly deceived. More responsibility was placed on Adam who completely understood what he was doing.

Estranged from Each Other

Read Genesis 3:7. After Adam and Eve ate the fruit, what did

they do? _____

An evident consequence of Adam and Eve's disobedience was the toll on their marital relationship. They noticed that they were naked and covered themselves with fig leaves. From whom were they hiding? They were hiding not only from God but also from each other. Immediately, guilt and shame entered into their open love relationship. Intimacy was gravely damaged. The loss of intimacy between men and women continues today, along with its accompanying maladies.

Read Genesis 3: 9-12. What was Adam's response when God confronted him with his disobedience? Check one or more.
☐ He blamed the animals.   ☐ He blamed God.
☐ He blamed Eve.

When God confronted Adam with his disobedience, Adam's answer was to blame his wife and then to blame God because He put Eve in the garden with him! I can just hear him say, *God, you know I love that woman, but I haven't been able to think straight since she came into my life. You are the One who gave her to me! Didn't You know she would cause me problems?*

Read Genesis 3:13. What was Eve's response when confronted?
☐ She blamed Adam.   ☐ She blamed the serpent.
☐ She blamed God.

Eve followed her husband's example. When things go wrong, we look for someone or something to blame. Eve chose to blame the serpent.

Disciplining our three children has been a challenge, especially when we didn't know who was in the wrong. One day David discovered that one of them had been disobedient. David lined up all three and starting with the oldest, asked, "Jonathan, did you do this?" Jonathan replied in a very serious voice, "No sir, I did not." David then asked Matthew, "Did you do this?" Matthew replied, "No sir, I did not." Amy was standing between her brothers, looking intently at them as they answered. When her turn came, she repeated the same words but with her hands nervously moving the whole time. We immediately knew the guilty one. At the sweet age of four, Amy was learning to avoid taking responsibility for her actions. Just like Amy, we each would rather someone else took the blame for our mistakes rather than admit failure.

The biblical record does not tell us the nature of Adam and Eve's relationship after they left Eden. We do know that they suffered punishment for their sin, just as we do today. The man would toil and struggle in his work, and what was meant to be pleasurable for the woman became painful instead. Eve would experience difficulties both bearing and rearing her children. Although "your desire will be for your husband" is interpreted in many ways, I believe it refers to the wife's desire to control and direct her husband's life. We see it first when Eve has Adam eat the fruit. Her original desire to encourage and support her husband, which was a wonderful source of ministry in his life, fell to a tendency to control.

To the woman he said,
"I will greatly increase your
pains in childbearing;
with pain you will give
birth to children.
Your desire will be for
your husband,
and he will rule over you."
Genesis 3:16

Restored by God

Adam and Eve had a broken relationship with God. We see a portrait of redemption as God covered them with skins (Gen. 3:21). Then God gave the first promise of the Savior who would defeat Satan.

How do you interpret Genesis 3:15? _____

_____

"I will put enmity
between you and the
woman,
and between your
offspring and hers;
he will crush your head,
and you will strike
his heel."
Genesis 3:15

The woman's "seed" (KJV) or "offspring" referred to Christ. In the third chapter of Genesis God alluded to a Savior whose blood sacrifice for sin had been ordained from the foundation, or beginning, of the world (v. 15). Satan would meet destruction by Christ's death on the cross! Hebrews 9:12

tells us, "Without the shedding of blood there is no forgiveness of sins." Only God can provide a substitute suitable to take the penalty for sin. We cannot pay the price through our own efforts.

If you have not made the decision to accept Christ's sacrifice on the cross as payment for your sins, please read "Reclaiming God's Perfect Plan" on page 25. If you are a Christian, you may feel you have not allowed God to restore completely your relationship with Him. You may not feel you have fully accepted His gracious offer of new life in Christ.

All of us have failed in many ways. Sometimes our mistakes overwhelm us, but God is seeking reconciliation. What sins do you feel keep you from fellowship with God? Confess these sins to God. Repentance means to turn around. Tell God you want to obey Him. Thank Him for His forgiveness.

Dear God, _____

_____

_____

Reclaiming God's Perfect Plan

Mankind's disobedience brought the curse of sin and death on Paradise, but Christ came to redeem us from that curse. If you have not trusted Jesus Christ as your Savior, there is no hope of reconciliation between you and God. There are no fig leaves that God will accept—no church membership, no good works, no being a nice wife and a good mother—none of our attempts to win God's favor will do. You must recognize that you are a sinner by nature and that the punishment for sin is death. Jesus Christ died in your place on the cross. Three days later He rose from the dead victorious over sin and death. He is the only substitute God will accept.

How does this personal relationship with Jesus Christ begin? Study the Bible verses in the margin. The payment due God for sin is death: separation forever from God. God loved us sinners so much that He gave His Son to die for our sins and give us eternal life. To have the new nature of Christ, you must believe that Jesus died for your sins and declare that you accept Him as Savior. This is God's promise to you—if you accept Jesus as your personal Savior, He will accept you.

Call on the Lord to save you now as you pray this prayer:

Dear God, I know I have sinned by breaking Your laws, and I ask for Your forgiveness. I believe that Jesus died for my sins. I want to receive new life in Him. I will follow Jesus as my Savior and attempt to obey Him in all that I do. In the name of Jesus I pray. Amen.

To grow in your new life in Christ, continue to cultivate this new relationship through reading the Bible, God's blueprint for a godly life; through a regular time of talking to God in prayer; and through fellowship with other Bible-believing Christians in a church near your home. As a disciple of Jesus, you will want to follow in His steps. Jesus' life was a life of service to others. You will want to find opportunities for service in your church and community.

Once you have received God's redemption, some profound changes will occur. Some of the effects of the curse will be removed from your life! When you trust Christ, you become a new creation (2 Cor. 5:17). Christ's indwelling presence through His Holy Spirit enables you to change habits and attitudes. He also transforms the way you view life. Genesis 1 and 2 help you understand what God had in mind for you in the first place. Then you can begin, by faith, to live that way right now.

All have sinned and fall short of the glory of God.
Romans 3:23

The wages of sin is death, but the gift of God is eternal life in Christ Jesus our Lord.
Romans 6:23

God demonstrates his own love for us in this: while we were still sinners, Christ died for us.
Romans 5:8

If you confess with your mouth, "Jesus is Lord," and believe in your heart that God raised him from the dead, you will be saved.
Romans 10:9

"Everyone who calls on the name of the Lord will be saved."
Romans 10:13

Day 5

The Source of Lasting Joy

"This is now bone of my bone and flesh of my flesh; she shall be called 'woman,' for she was taken out of man." Genesis 2:23

Are you redeemed? Yes, you are if you have trusted Jesus Christ as your Lord and Savior. Once you've received God's redemption, you can begin the restoration of your marriage towards God's original design. God's Spirit will transform your mind, bring health to your emotions, and redirect your will. He will breathe new life into your spirit. He will define and develop your special and exalted role as a suitable helper.

The Source of Misery

For the most part, I would describe the early years of my marriage as happy. It was a time of new beginnings, a new ministry, a new home, and a beautiful baby. We weren't wealthy, but all our needs were met.

When I eventually found myself very unhappy, I was taken by surprise. Although I knew God had called me into missionary service, the stress of moving to the Philippines seemed to strangle all the happiness out of me. We were in a new culture and country; learning a second language proved to be more difficult than I ever imagined. My husband was out of the house each day using the language and ministering to people. I was at home just trying to survive. Daily life was a struggle.

To top it all off, Matthew didn't sleep all night for the first year—and his brother was a two-year-old! I had no friend to talk to in order to work out my frustrations. I was lonely and sad. At times, I found myself being angry at my husband because he was supposed to make me happy.

I had a lot of growing up to do. I realized that I was still caught up in my youthful dreams of "they lived happily ever after." Happiness is an emotion that comes and goes depending on circumstances. When I experienced difficult circumstances, I found myself filled with sadness.

As I spent much time praying, God confirmed that no matter what was going on around me, He had provided a way for me to find joy in the midst of my circumstances. That promise doesn't always mean the circumstances will change; sometimes God changes us. Many of you may be thinking, *I'm not the one who needs to change! Why does God always want the woman to change?* It isn't that God wants one person over another to change, but He wants you to find that deep abiding peace and joy that is not depleted by circumstances or trials.

Joy is more a part of our character—who we are—rather than an emotion. It cannot be dependent on circumstances because circumstances change. Your husband could lose his job, your child could be injured, or conflict could occur in a significant relationship. Finding lasting joy, then, is not so much finding a feeling but finding Someone! We cannot will ourselves to experience joy; it results from a deep spiritual encounter.

 Read Philippians 4:1-4. Paul says we are to rejoice in what (v. 4)?
- [ ] peaceful circumstances
- [ ] children
- [ ] husband
- [ ] the Lord

Look to the Lord as your Source of joy.

The Philippian Christians brought great joy to Paul. They ministered to him in so many ways that he said, "I thank my God every time I remember you" (Phil. 1:3). However, two women in the church were arguing.

 In Philippians 4:1-4, what does Paul ask the women to do?

_____

Paul exhorted them to agree with each other. In other words, they were to find common ground. Paul encouraged the other Christians to help them in this effort. Then Paul appears to change the conversation. He says to "rejoice in the Lord always. I will say it again: Rejoice!"

 If you were advising the Philippians, how is joy possible in the midst of conflict? Write your answer in the margin.

To have joy in your outward life, your inward life must rejoice in the Lord always. According to Philippians 4:5-9, joy is a by-product of
- gentleness—a kind and compassionate spirit
- awareness of the Lord's presence and anticipation of His second coming
- prayer—petitioning God for what we need
- thanksgiving—having a grateful spirit
- focusing thoughts on things that build up, not tear down
- practicing godly living modeled in the life of Paul and others.

My brothers, you whom I love and long for, my joy and crown, that is how you should stand firm in the Lord, dear friends!

I plead with Euodia and I plead with Syntyche to agree with each other in the Lord. Yes, and I ask you, loyal yokefellow, help these women who have contended at my side in the cause of the gospel, along with Clement and the rest of my fellow workers, whose names are in the book of life.

Rejoice in the Lord always, I will say it again: Rejoice!
Philippians 4:1-4

Joy results from putting our focus on God rather than on ourselves, others, and circumstances. An intimate relationship with the Lord—spending time in prayer and fellowship—leads to peace in our inner lives. Then we will be anxious for nothing (4:6).

The Lord blesses us with joy in marriage.

Not only is the Lord our Source of joy, but He also blesses us with joy in our marriages. In the Hebrew, Genesis 2:23 is said with great excitement. I like the way this verse reads in the *Living Bible*. After God brings the woman to him, Adam exclaims, "This is it!" Today, a man might say, *God, she is exactly what I need and want!*

Adam realized Eve had been made by God, given to him by God, and designed especially for his needs. Small wonder we read of his excitement. This tender and touching scene reminds us that love flourishes in God's original design. The woman is valued and honored alongside the man. The man finds completeness in the woman. Neither was possible without God's master plan.

God is in the business of miracles, and He designed your marriage to be a place where joy is found. The joy in my marriage began to return when I realized my security and joy had to come from the Lord. When I released David from the responsibility of my happiness, I truly began to experience the deep abiding peace and joy that only the Lord can give! The joy in my marriage was reinstated, and my love for my husband increased. In return, my husband's visible love for me also increased.

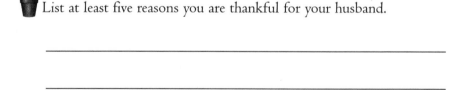 List at least five reasons you are thankful for your husband.

_____

_____

This week I want you to verbally thank your husband for one of the reasons you listed. Write his response in the margin beside your list.

Your marriage will turn a vital corner when you accept the truth that God can bring joy and intimacy to your marriage. No doubt you have different temperaments, interests, perspectives, tastes, abilities, personalities, and moods. These differences add variety and color to your marriage. Often we react to them as liabilities rather than assets. When differences cause conflict, it is not always easy to obey God's Word.

Read Ephesians 4:29-32. What are some inappropriate responses to

conflict in marriage? _____

_____

God desires that we have joy within our marriages, and He will show us how this can be a part of our lives if we will just be obedient to His principles.

Read James 1:2-4. James, the brother of Christ, wrote that we are to rejoice when we encounter trials. What good results come from

enduring trials? _____

_____

Trials will come, but through them we have the opportunity to become more dependent on God. Are you experiencing a trial right now? Will you give this trial to the Lord and not take it back out of His hands? Just leave it there and trust Him to do a mighty work. Write out your prayer giving God the situation with which you are having difficulty. Expect inner joy to result!

Dear God, _____   _____   _____

Do not let any unwholesome talk come out of your mouths, but only what is helpful for building others up according to their needs, that it may benefit those who listen. And do not grieve the Holy Spirit of God, with whom you were sealed for the day of redemption. Get rid of all bitterness, rage and anger, brawling and slander, along with every form of malice. Be kind and compassionate to one another, forgiving each other, just as in Christ God forgave you.
Ephesians 4:29-32

Consider it pure joy, my brothers, whenever you face trials of many kinds, because you know that the testing of your faith develops persever-ance. Perseverance must finish its work so that you may be mature and complete, not lacking anything.
James 1:2-4

[1]Ed Wheat, M.D. and Gloria Okes Perkins, *Love Life for Every Married Couple* (Grand Rapids: Zondervan Publishing House, 1980), 31.
[2]William F. Harley, Jr., *His Needs Her Needs* (Grand Rapids: Baker Book House Company, 1993), 10.

Week Two
Unfailing Love

This week you will identify

- how your belief about love compares to God's view of love;
- practical principles about giving and receiving love;
- ways to build affection and friendship;
- steps to nurture romantic love;
- the level of your *agape* love for your husband.

The psalmist called on God to help him because of God's unfailing love (Ps. 44:26). God's love never fails. Human love often fails, yet all of us long for unfailing love in marriage. How do we find a love that lasts, a love that endures all things (I Cor. 13:7)?

One of the main reasons we marry involves our need for love and intimacy. The relationship of husband and wife can be a deeply satisfying closeness of the mind, heart, body, and spirit. Unfortunately, the fact that we are married does not guarantee the delights of intimacy. The covers of women's magazines indicate that many couples find it difficult to achieve this intimacy. Yet all of us expect it, and without it, marriages often disintegrate. Even in stable marriages, couples will often admit that there is an emptiness in the core of their relationship because one or both of them don't know how to become intimate lovers.

You can be the happy exception! In a world of empty relationships, you can experience growing intimacy with your husband. The key to developing this type of relationship is found by understanding God's intention in marriage and by making choices to cultivate love.

Love is more than an emotional response. You must make a mental decision to love someone with unfailing love—even if the other person does not respond in kind. You must promote intimacy through loving actions and give love the chance to grow. Remember that this study is about women making a difference in marriage. You can provide an emotional climate that will nurture intimacy in your marriage.

A personal relationship with the Lord is the most important key in establishing intimacy within marriage. Without the Lord, perseverance is almost impossible. Without the Lord, negative thoughts will consume us. Without the Lord, our unmet needs will dominate our agendas. Without the Lord, we will look to our husbands to meet our love needs. Our husbands were not designed to meet our entire need for love. Expecting them to do so creates an environment of resentment and mistrust.

Part of God's purpose for wives is to reflect His love to our husbands. God cannot physically wrap His arms around our husbands, but we can! Let me challenge you to experience God's love on a daily basis! Then you will have His love to give to others!

Day 1
God's Truths about Love

Dear friends, let us love one another, for love comes from God. 1 John 4:7

Pam was stuck in a loveless marriage. The first time I talked to her she said, "I don't think it's possible for me to ever love my husband again. In fact, I don't know if I want to. At one time I would have been willing to work on my marriage, but everything inside me is dead!"

Although her husband was physically faithful, Frank was emotionally distant. For years she had tried to break down the wall between them. Now, she did not want to try—even one more time; she was ready to leave her marriage. Frank was begging her for one more chance. He claimed he was willing to do anything to save his marriage.

As I shared with Pam biblical insights about love, she agreed to apply God's principles to her marriage even though she felt no love for Frank. When I talked with her again later, she was ecstatic! She actually had felt a beginning spark of love in her heart for her husband.

Only God can put love in a heart when it's nowhere to be found! When we know God's Word and begin to apply it in daily situations, we can build, nurture, or restore love in our marriages. We can replace false beliefs with God's truths about love.

Beliefs from our Families

In your childhood you learned about love from your family. In my family of origin, my father often kissed my mother and proclaimed to all five children that we had the most beautiful mother in the whole world. My parents never fought in front of us. Therefore, I concluded that a loving husband would always kiss me before leaving the house, compliment me in front of others, and never argue with me.

Although I learned some truth about love from my parents, I also developed some wrong impressions. Yes, we are to be affirming with our words, but is it true that we never disagree? Definitely not, or God would not have spent so much time in the Scripture telling us how to resolve disagreements!

We may conclude that our spouses don't love us because they don't act like our dads or other significant others.

When we marry, we may conclude that our spouses don't love us because they don't act like our dads or other significant others. Love can be expressed in many ways. Find out as much as possible about how your husband's family expressed love. Was it physical with lots of hugs and kisses or shown through gifts or thoughtful deeds? Possibly it was by their spoken words or quality time spent together as a family. You will develop significant insight into your husband's behavior by studying his family's interactions.

 Who were your husband's role models for love and marriage? How have these individuals influenced his behavior toward you?

_____

_____

Many women grew up in homes with sexual, emotional, or physical abuse. Their definition of love may be distorted; they may view sexual love as dirty or cruel; they may feel no one can be trusted.

My heart aches for those I counsel who have experienced some type of childhood abuse. Only by God's power and His healing words in Scripture can one who has experienced abuse begin to rebuild her life. If you have experienced abuse, my prayers are that God will surround you with His loving arms around you and that you will experience His love! He has given you the Holy Spirit as Comforter. He will never, ever leave you!

God is a God of miracles, and He can bring good out of bad situations! Don't let what you learned as a child keep you from experiencing the fullness of God's love in your marriage!

Beliefs from Past Experiences

Donna fell in love at the age of 15 and planned to get married immediately after high school graduation. She dropped all of her friends and focused her attention and energy on this wonderful guy. They did get married, but soon there were problems.

Donna found out that her husband was unfaithful. Even on the night before they were married, he was with another woman. After she could no longer take his unfaithfulness, they divorced. The pain of this betrayal left Donna with a deep distrust of all men.

Not all men are unfaithful. We must guard against false conclusions that come from bad experiences. Christ understands our hurts. He suffered extreme pain as He hung on the cross for our sins. He was ridiculed, physically abused, and degraded. Just as someday Jesus will be lifted up to receive the praise of all mankind, God will also lift up and defend those who have suffered unjustly. Will you give your hurts to the Lord and allow Him to bring healing to your life?

 List a specific hurt you would like to give to the Lord today.

Beliefs from Culture

Advertisers appeal to our need for love. The world consistently tells us what love is, where we can find it, what we can buy to attract it, and who we must be to deserve it. Television, movies, and magazines portray love as an irrational feeling beyond our control. From the media, a woman could easily assume that unless she is slim, wears a certain brand of jeans, or smells of just the right perfume, she has little chance for love. Of course, this love is strictly based on physical appeal and lasts only until the next love interest appears.

The dictionary has over 25 definitions of love. Love has been called the most elusive emotion in the world. The more you try to attract and keep it, the more it seems to allude you. Men and women are so desperate for love that they willingly settle for substitutes.

 Will you ask God to reveal the lies of culture that you believe? These lies may feel very comfortable, like longtime friends. Ask God to give you a willing heart to reject all of your lies and then to replace them with His truth. List these lies in the margin.

Beliefs from God's Word.

In week I we studied God's plan for marriage. He created marriage as a one-flesh relationship (Gen. 2:23). When He brought Eve to Adam, Adam was overwhelmed with God's good gift. Satan, on the other hand,

The wrath of God is being revealed from heaven against all the godlessness and wickedness of men who suppress the truth by their wickedness, since what may be known about God is plain to them, because God has made it plain to them. For since the creation of the world God's invisible qualities—his eternal power and divine nature—have been clearly seen, being understood from what has been made, so that men are without excuse. ... They exchanged the truth of God for a lie, and worshiped and served created things rather than the Creator—who is forever praised.
Romans 1:18-20,25

distorted God's truth. One of the results of sin entering the world was the devastating impact on the relationship between Adam and Eve. They clothed themselves as a recognition that they could no longer function without shame and guilt. Adam blamed Eve. Truth was now replaced with lies.

 Read Romans 1:18-20, 25. What results when we replace God's truth with lies (v. 25)?

_____

God abandoned the people because they had first abandoned His truth. If we want God's power released to work in our marriages, we must confront the lies we have believed and replace them with God's truth. Tomorrow we will look at the foundational principles of God's love. Today we want to remind ourselves of the source of love.

 Read I John 4:7-12 in your Bible. Love comes from what source?

_____

Is God's love based on our response? ☐ yes ☐ no

How are we to show our love for God (v. 11)? _____

_____

The Bible is a love story. God loves you so much that He sent His only Son to die on a cross for you. His love does not vary from day to day depending on your response. His love has no limit—you can't use up your supply. His love has no end—it's eternal.

If you want to give and receive real love, you must begin with God and discover from His Word how much He loves you. Love recognizes the unique value of its beloved. You were created in God's image, and He loves you greatly. You, in turn, have been given God's Spirit so that you can love others—even those who do not always treat you kindly.

Loving others, including our spouses, is one of the most difficult steps of obedience. Sometimes love for our spouses can only come from Almighty God. Love is possible when "God lives in us and His love is made complete in us" (4:12). Have you tried to love your spouse in your own strength or based on his behavior toward you? Have you allowed God to love your spouse through you? Read 1 John 4:19-21 in the margin. Substitute the word *husband* for the word *brother*. Does reading the passage with the substitution make a difference in your perspective? Today will you ask for a renewed love for your spouse?

We love because he first loved us. If anyone says, "I love God," yet hates his brother, he is a liar. For anyone who does not love his brother, whom he has seen, cannot love God, whom he has not seen. And he has given us this command: Whoever loves God must also love his brother.
1 John 4:19-21

Dear God, _____

_____

_____

Day 2
Principles of Marital Love

Dear friends, since God so loved us, we also ought to love one another.
1 John 4:11

Yesterday we examined lies that keep us from experiencing and giving God's love. Today we will establish foundational principles about love from God's Word. The first principle may sound elementary, but I feel it's essential to state as we begin.

Love is a choice.
Recall from day 1 that Satan distorts what God creates. He would like for you to believe that love is an irrational feeling outside your control—that love just happens with no warning. According to this theory, if you are attracted to a married man or he is attracted to you, you are helpless to stop it. You are a victim of your own passions.

According to God's Word, love doesn't just mysteriously happen. We are not victims but actors in the drama of love. Just as we choose to love initially, we can choose to continue to love.

God's love for Israel, His chosen people, was just that—a choice. He chose them despite their lack of loveliness. In fact, He chose to love

"I will establish my covenant as an everlasting covenant between me and you and your descendants after you for the generations to come, to be your God and the God of your descendants after you. The whole land of Canaan, where you are now an alien, I will give as an everlasting possession to you and your descendants after you; and I will be their God."

Genesis 17:7-8

The Lord appeared to us in the past, saying:
"I have loved you with an everlasting love;
I have drawn you with loving-kindness."

Jeremiah 31:3

them before they were born (see Gen. 17:7-8 in the margin). God's love for Israel was purposeful and deliberate.

Read Jeremiah 31:3. How did God describe His love? (check one or more)

☐ tentative   ☐ everlasting

☐ based on appearance   ☐ nurtured by lovingkindness

Love requires nurture.

My daughter takes piano lessons. The more difficult songs to play are often the songs she loves the most because she has given them time and attention. Love is costly and requires patience. Even in the most difficult circumstances, love can grow and develop into something beautiful.

When I first married, I thought that since my husband and I were Christians, we would automatically have intimate love in our marriage. It didn't take long for my selfish desires to return from the honeymoon. I wanted things to go my way. After years of struggle, when I learned that God wanted me to give love 100 percent of the time, no matter what my husband did, I was faced with a choice. Did I want to show love to my husband even when he was very unloveable? When I was able to submit to God's authority and live in obedience to Him, my love for David grew. I learned to nurture that love.

If given the choice of going back in time in my marriage, I would choose to remain right where I am. The love we have now is so much deeper and more intimate than ever before. It still takes hard work and patience—lots of patience! The result is a wonderfully kind and intimate marriage that I could not have imagined!

What are some ways we nurture love in marriage? Be prepared to

share your ideas with your group. _____

_____

Thoughts affect feelings.

As you change your thoughts to align to God's truth, you will find God faithful to help you change your behavior. Loving behavior must begin with loving thoughts. Thoughts affect your feelings. Our feelings about our husbands will show through no matter what words we speak. We must examine our hearts and focus on the loving thoughts that God intends for us.

Probably more than any other area, I struggle with my thought life. Thoughts affect the way we see people and circumstances, and they also have a direct impact on our communication and behavior. If you tell your husband you love him, yet you harbor anger in your heart, which message do you think he receives? Probably the anger. Who we are on the inside always has a way of showing up on the outside.

🏺 Underline types of memories that diminish rather than build love.

past mistakes	helpful deeds	grievances	suspicions
kindnesses	omissions	family outings	quarrels

Have you ever found yourself getting angry at someone about an event that happened many years before? How does that happen? We have to dwell on the event until those painful memories are stirred from ashes to bright embers. If you spend your days concentrating on ways your husband has failed you, you will not grow in love. You will grow in resentment and anger.

Spend time remembering positive experiences that drew you to your husband. Make a mental list of qualities that first attracted you to your beloved. Anticipate future pleasures with your mate. Give up any outside attachments or daydreams about someone else.

🏺 What does Matthew 15:18-19 say about the origin of our words and actions?

_____

_____

"The things that come out of the mouth come from the heart, and these make a man 'unclean.' For out of the heart come evil thoughts, murder, adultery, sexual immorality, theft, false testimony, slander."
Matthew 15:18-19

Changing our thoughts is an essential step that comes before changing our words or deeds. How do we change our thoughts? James 4:8-9 instructs us to purify our hearts by mourning our sins. Then we are told in Philippians 4:8 to replace sinful thoughts with thoughts that are worthy of our new life in Christ.

Whatever is true, whatever is noble, whatever is right, whatever is pure, whatever is lovely, whatever is admirable—if anything is excellent or praiseworthy—think about such things.
Philippians 4:8

Underline what we are to think about according to Philippians 4:8.

Jesus pointed to the heart as the source of either good or evil (Matt. 15:18-20). I find it essential to daily confess any wrong thinking and ask for God's help as I pray Psalms 19:14.

Read Psalm 19:14. Let these words inspire your time of prayer.

May the words of my mouth and the meditation of my heart be pleasing in your sight, O Lord, my Rock and my Redeemer.
Psalm 19:14

| Dear God, _____ |
| _____ |
| _____ |

Day 3

Affection and Friendship

Whoever loves God must also love his brother. 1 John 4:21

Love, one of the most unusual words in the English language, is used to describe our feelings about food, sports, vacations, children, and husbands. During New Testament times, the Greek language was used throughout the Roman Empire. The Greeks used several words for love to distinguish its many facets. These words represented affection, or family love; friendship love; erotic or passionate love; and God's love.

The remainder of this week, we will examine these varied types of love, which are important ingredients in a well-rounded relationship. Is your love for your husband mostly affection or family love? Are you and he best friends? Do you enjoy a passionate relationship? Like a multi-faceted diamond, marital love is best expressed in many dimensions.

Affection

Family love is the natural affection that occurs between family members. It is the sense of belonging to each other that gives us security and acceptance. This love is supportive, encouraging, and comforting. I like the way the Amplified Bible translates Romans 12:10: "Love one another with brotherly affection [as members of one family], giving precedence and showing honor to one another."

Believers are to love one another just as family members love each other. Paul encouraged it among the believers at Thessalonica: "Now about brotherly love we do not need to write to you, for you yourselves have been taught by God to love each other. And in fact, you do love all the brothers ... Yet we urge you, brothers, to do so more and more" (I Thess. 4:9-10). This is how we all want to be loved by our church family, but it needs to extend to our individual families, as well.

We were gentle among you, like a mother caring for her little children. We loved you so much that we were delighted to share with you not only the gospel of God but our lives as well, because you had become so dear to us.

1 Thessalonians 2:7-8

Affection gives its life in true devotion to the one it loves. Read I Thessalonians 2:7-8. To what image does Paul compare his love for the Thessalonians? (check one)

☐ a husband for his wife   ☐ a nursing mother for her child
☐ a lover for his beloved

My heart cries out for those who grew up in families without natural affection for one another. In homes where natural affection is lacking, the incidence of abuse is higher. A sexual abuser has no love for a child that supercedes his or her own needs and lusts. God's Word clearly shows in both the Old and New Testaments that incest is wrong. If you have endured this experience, find a Christian counselor or godly woman to whom you can turn for counsel. If you have not been abused, ask God if He would have you befriend someone who has gone through this experience. Perhaps you can point her to the only Source of healing and acceptance.

I cannot imagine living in a home without natural affection. However, many homes lack this type of love. Marriages can benefit from cultivating family oneness.

Affection shows itself in practical ways. When my husband and I were having church in our home and I was working full time, I would often come home from work to find a meeting in progress in my home. Knowing that it was important to me that our home was presentable, David always picked up before people started arriving. This was a practical oneness. We were working together to achieve mutual goals.

What is a practical way you can show affection to your husband? Write your answer in the margin.

Affection is an encouraging love. It believes in the loved one. It offers refuge to a husband, so he can forget the difficulties of the world. This love adds security to a relationship. The fact that you are available to your husband no matter what may happen can help him to persevere during trying circumstances. Does your husband know that no matter what happens, you are there for him?

When your husband comes home after a difficult day at work, is your home a tranquil place where he can find peace and rest? Or, do you immediately confront him with all the problems of the day and demand that he respond?

Our husbands are very vulnerable when they experience a job setback. At these times we can really be supportive and show affection by not criticizing or using those dreadful words, "I told you so." View setbacks and disappointments as a time that you can show, beyond a shadow of doubt, your devotion to your husband.

 What are some ways you can encourage your husband? _____

_____

Oh ladies, God has given you a special role to support and build the self-esteem of your mate. I have heard many men state that their wives helped them to become the man God intended. To what type of man do you want to be married? Then treat your man just like that! Affection is essential to a marriage. It protects the husband's heart and provides a home to which he wants to return. Take seriously your responsibility to show affection for your husband.

Friendship Love

Jesus and His disciples modeled friendship love. Peter expressed his love for Jesus: "Lord, You know everything; that I love You [that I have a deep, instinctive, personal affection for You, as for a close friend]" (John 21:17, AMP). In John 13:23, John, who called himself the disciple whom Jesus loved, leaned against Him, possibly with his head on His chest. Only friends would enjoy this close association.

Friendship love is also important in marriage. Have you ever said, "My husband is my best friend"? Friendship love requires enjoyable interaction—giving as well as receiving. It speaks of affection, fondness, or liking. Friendship love responds to kindness and appreciation.

Read Titus 2:4. What are more experienced wives instructed to do?

They can train the younger women to love their husbands and children.
Titus 2:4

_____

If friendship love is to be taught, that means it can be learned! Just as you can learn relationship skills for friendships with other women, you can learn to be a friend to your husband.

Developing a friendship relationship with your husband **first** requires spending time with each other. Just being together, regardless of the activity, probably characterized your dating. How long has it been since you did something fun with your husband? Find common ground or seek to develop an interest in what your husband likes to do. I have a dear friend who took up golf so she could spend time with her husband. They now play about three times a week. Does she love the game of golf? No, but she loves being with her husband and would not exchange this time for anything!

Does your husband know that you desire to be with him above all others, or does he sense that you are with him only out of responsibility or necessity? Your words, as well as your actions, reveal your inner motivations. Carefully choose your words and facial expressions. Make sure your face says the same thing as your words!

 Does your husband know that you enjoy doing things with him? (circle)   yes   no

If not, how will you choose to let him know? _____

_____

What mutually-enjoyable experience will you suggest to him this week? Write several ideas in the margin.

Second, communicate with each other. Taking time to talk is essential to building a friendship. Communication involves committing to expressing your thoughts and feelings.

My dear brothers, take note of this: Everyone should be quick to listen, slow to speak and slow to become angry.
James 1:19

 What communication advice does James 1:19 give?

_____

**Developing
Friendship Love**
1. Spend time together.
2. Communicate with
   each other.
3. Trust each other.

Third, friendship love trusts each other. Jonathan, son of King Saul, and David, future king of Israel, were great friends. "The soul of Jonathan was knit with the soul of David and Jonathan loved him as his own soul" (I Sam. 18:1, KJV). David and Jonathan cherished their friendship and trusted their lives to each other (I Sam. 20:12-17). Because you cherish your husband, you are loyal and committed to this relationship. If your husband tells you something in confidence, can he trust that you will tell no one else?

The husband of the virtuous woman trusted his wife (Prov. 31:11). When a husband trusts his wife, he knows that no matter what happens, they will face it together; he feels successful no matter what happens in the job market. Does your husband trust you? Does he know that you don't criticize him in front of friends or in front of your children? When we are angry, we often try to lower the estimation others have of the person with whom we are angry. We may subconsciously want our children to think less of their dads. Is this morally right? Not at all. Show your commitment to your husband individually, but also show your commitment to your husband in front of others.

 Evaluate your friendship love with your husband.

weak friendship   friends most of the time   strong friendship

Developing a friendship with your husband also involves getting to know him better. Isn't it sad when a husband and wife live together for a lifetime but never really ever come to know each other? Unfortunately, this is true all too often. Let me challenge you to sit down with your husband with the following questions that are designed to help you know each other's hearts.

1. What has been the hardest experience of your life?
2. What has been the happiest time of your life?
3. What are your deepest fears?
4. If you could be guaranteed success, what would you do?
5. What qualities do you appreciate in a friend?
6. What activities bring you the most satisfaction?

Oh ladies, we need to study our husbands. We need to listen not only to their words, but also to their nonverbal cues. Can you honestly say that you can tell just by looking at your husband whether he is tired, upset, or frustrated? If not, begin the careful study of your husband. Above all else, seek to be the friend to your husband that you would like to have in him. Pray today for God to increase your friendship love.

Dear God, _____

_____

_____

Day 4
Rekindle Romance

We love because he first loved us. 1 John 4:19

Throughout the New Testament, we are taught to love each other. If we love our brothers and sisters in Christ, how much more should we show love to our husbands? Many times we go out of our way to love others but leave our husbands with the leftover energy and passion. God has given us the responsibility to love our husbands. This is a lifetime responsibility nurtured through time and communication.

Today we are going to look at romantic love. We are not talking about physical sexual love, although romance often leads in that direction. We will spend an entire week on sexual love (see week 7). Sex is not the most important aspect of your marriage, but it is an indicator of its health. Difficulty in the sexual area is usually a symptom of another problem.

This special gift from God to us is to be expressed only within marriage. He created it, and He only created what was "very good" (Gen. 1:31). Some Christians say that romance is just the whipping cream on the sundae and not essential at all. I believe they are wrong. In Genesis 2, Adam and Eve fit perfectly together in every realm. They were to be one emotionally, spiritually, mentally, and also physically.

Romance is often the starting point for marriage. The emotions of romantic love can give a person a sense of well-being and a new outlook on life. This love is dependent upon the response of the other person. It takes two people for romantic love to continue. If romantic love is not returned, this love can die. Although romantic love is not mentioned in the New Testament, it can add excitement to your marriage! It promotes an atmosphere which leads to mutual fulfillment—sexual and otherwise.

Let's think about the various climates that are essential to developing and sustaining romantic love.

The Mental Climate

Romance begins in the brain! Recall from day 2 that love is a choice. Romance is also a choice. We must make a decision to allow ourselves to become passionate about an object or a person. Daily we choose to come into a closer relationship with our spouses or to give in to the temptations to be selfish, which pulls us apart and increases the distance between us.

 Read Ephesians 4:22-24. List what we are to put off, to discard.

_____

You were taught, with regard to your former way of life, to put off your old self, which is being corrupted by its deceitful desires; to be made new in the attitude of your minds; and to put on the new self, created to be like God in true righteousness and holiness.
Ephesians 4:22-24

We are to discard our old selves which are corrupted by deceitful desires. If allowed to run unchecked in a marriage, these self-centered desires can eventually destroy it. Perhaps you are thinking, *I'd like for my spouse to change first, and then I will be responsive to his needs.* Or maybe you feel you have so many pressures that you don't have the mental energy to focus on someone else's needs.

The Greek word for *corrupt (phtheiro)* has three graphic meanings: *shrivel, wither,* and *spoil.* If self-centered desires take over, our marriage relationship may shrivel from lack of attention or wither from the coldness in the relationship. When I think of something spoiling, I think of my refrigerator. Often I have a wonderful dish of food I forget and leave in the back of my refrigerator; of course, it spoils because I have ignored its presence. How often do we ignore our husbands? We feel that we have many more pressing things to take care of—children, jobs, housework, and church responsibilities. We become so self-centered that we forget the most important earthly relationship that God has given us.

God gives us the ability to discard behaviors which lead to destruction. The Phillip's translation says, "Fling off the dirty clothes of the old way of living." We need to fling off the old ways of thinking and replace them with God's priorities.

What thinking patterns can you put off, making way for romance to grow between you and your husband? (check one or more)
- [ ] I'm too busy.
- [ ] He doesn't deserve my attention.
- [ ] I need to be cared for instead.

Ephesians 4:22-24 tells us to be constantly renewed in the spirit of our minds, having a fresh mental and spiritual attitude. I like how Phillips translates it, "Put on the clean fresh clothes of the new life which was made by God's design." God says, *Put it on.* Choose to do it, and God will give you the power to accomplish it.

As we allow God to keep our minds fresh and renewed with the positive counsel from the Scriptures, then we will be able to make right choices in our marriages. Sometimes we allow the routine of marriage and the responsibilities of family to dull our sensitivities towards developing romance with our husbands. As God leads us, we will see our God-given priorities and we will not overlook our relationship with our husbands. You must look at your behavior and ask yourself the following question: Will this build romance into our marriage or tear it down?

Which of your behaviors build up romance in your marriage? What about your behaviors or responses that inhibit romance? List both types below.

Behaviors that build	Behaviors that inhibit

Let me address the possibility that your partner may not be willing to respond to your desire to enhance the romance in your marriage.

First, you must approach your husband with sensitivity, not trying to push him into something for which he is not ready. Take it slowly, with patience and with prayer. God can slowly break through the barrier that may have built up over the years.

Second, allow God to transform your mind so that you are not just seeking something you want, but you are seeking what is best for your husband. You truly want him to know that you love him and that you desire an intimate relationship with him just because of who he is. Don't allow your fantasies of that ideal man to be the motivating factor in your response to your husband. Ask God to transform your mind to do His "good, pleasing and perfect will" (Rom. 12:2).

The Emotional Climate

Intimacy and romance in marriage can be yours if you choose to pursue them. Pursue them patiently, consistently, and delicately, with sensitivity. Nothing is more vulnerable to fluctuations, changes, and influences—positive or negative—than your intimate relationship with your husband. The second climate in developing romance in our marriages is to provide the right emotional climate for love to grow. This climate is fueled by shared feelings and experiences.

If the chill of misunderstanding or the heat of annoyance threatens your closeness, forgive freely and be quick to reconcile. Show your willingness to be romantic with your husband by forgiving him and letting him know that you desire him. Remove roadblocks of anger and bitterness which prevent a person from experiencing love and romance. When we allow anger and bitterness to build up, we are actually becoming very self-oriented. We care more about our rights and our hurts than we do about developing our capacity to love as God loves.

This climate is fueled by shared feelings and experiences.

Do emotional barriers keep you from experiencing romance

in your marriage? If so, list them._____

_____

What one thing could you do in the following week that would

begin tearing down these barriers? _____

The Physical Climate

The third step in developing romance in your marriage is physical touching. I am not referring to sexual touching—just that pat on the shoulder or hand on the knee that says *I love you.* Studies indicate that we need 10 meaningful touches per day. Giving your mate physical attention includes sexual touching, such as holding hands, hugging, and kissing; touch builds romance in a marriage.

Practice giving your mate eye contact. Studies show that couples who are deeply in love have more eye contact than other couples. An old song says, "I only have eyes for you." Your eyes can signal romantic interest and add color to your marriage. Have you ever been in a crowded room and caught the eye of your beloved? Volumes of words are said with that one glance. Today, will you start really looking at your husband? Look at him with the eyes of one who is in love. Seek to make eye contact with a look that says, "I can't wait to be alone with you."

The key ingredient in romance is time to be alone! Put the children to bed early, have a candle-lit dinner, or sit outside in the moonlight. Plan an evening away or in a special hotel. The possibilities are limited only by your imagination. One of my favorite alone times with David involves having coffee in an outdoor garden where violin and piano music plays softly in the background. Sometimes the words are few, sometimes they are many, but we are able to enjoy being alone with each other.

Above all, stop nagging! Nagging, griping, or complaining can squelch any interest in being romantic. This is a must! If nagging is a problem for you, the Lord may want you to spend some time in prayer about this habit. If not, pray for motivation to stimulate romance in your marriage.

Climates for Growing Love
1. Mental Climate: ask God to transform your mind to do His will
2. Emotional Climate: remove roadblocks such as feelings of anger and bitterness.
3. Physical Climate: practice physical touches with your husband daily.

Dear God, _____

_____

_____

Day 5

The Greatest Love

Whoever does not love does not know God, because God is love. 1 John 4:8

If your marriage lacks love, God has provided a solution! *Agape* is the Greek word that describes God's love for us. This love is fueled not by emotions but by will, and it can be demonstrated by one person. When we practice *agape*, God supplies the resources out of His own nature.

▓ Read Romans 5:6-8. Underline the proof of God's *agape* love.

God desires that *agape* love characterize our lives. He is the one who makes this love grow through His gift of the Holy Spirit. Growth is not automatic, but when in obedience to God's will we choose to show love, even without the accompanying feelings, a miracle happens! Love swells in our hearts until we have to share this overflow with others.

Agape love is unconditional.

Many of you were raised in homes where your parents' love was conditional. "I will show my love to you if … you make good grades. … you always obey. … you are quiet when adults are around. … you don't embarrass me in front of my friends." Many wives also show conditional love to their spouses. "I will show love to you if you show it first. We will have sex tonight if you.… I will love you if you go to church with me." Conditional love sends a message that you believe your partner has to do something to be worthy of your love.

Agape love is unconditional. God extends His love to sinners. Because you are empowered by God, you are not limited in how much *agape* love you can give. Your supply is not dependent on your husband deserving your love. You know that you do not deserve God's love, yet He sent His Son to die on a cross for your sins.

Your husband may have many unlovely qualities, but you don't have to feel love before you show love. You may have to act out of obedience to God because the feelings or the desire to love isn't there. God will love through you out of His power and strength.

Would you ask God to help you see your husband as He does? God sees someone who has insecurities, needs, fears, aspirations, and hopes

You see, at just the right time, when we were still powerless, Christ died for the ungodly. Very rarely will anyone die for a righteous man, though for a good man someone might possibly dare to die. But God demonstrates his own love for us in this: While we were still sinners, Christ died for us.
Romans 5:6-8

for the future. By loving our husbands unconditionally, we protect their hearts.

Evaluate your unconditional love by circling *yes* or *no*.

- Is your treatment of your husband usually based on his behavior?
  yes   no
- Does your husband's performance determine the degree of love you give him?   yes   no
- Is your love based on a 50/50 relationship?   yes   no
- Do you think that love should be shown only as a reward for good behavior?   yes   no
- Do you feel that your partner has to change before you can love him more?   yes   no
- Do you think you can improve your partner's behavior by withholding love?   yes   no

Agape love is unconditional. Jesus Christ is our example. With full knowledge of how sinful we would be, He died on the cross for us before we were born! How can we apply Christ's sacrifice to our marriages? Because *agape* love wants the best for the other person, it's able to keep on giving even if nothing is received in return. God calls us to put all our disappointments and desires aside and allow His mighty love to increase and overflow (1 Thess. 3:12). We can live a life of love because we are being rooted and established in love (Eph. 3:17).

The Love Chapter

First Corinthians 13 is well known for Paul's beautiful language and high ideals concerning love. Paul said becoming loving people exceeds being busy. The preceding verse states, "Now I will show you the most excellent way." Notice it says the most excellent way, not one out of many.

The word *love* in 1 Corinthians 13 is not romantic love, nor is it deep affection or friendship love. Paul is talking about *agape*, or God's love.

Read 1 Corinthians 13:4-7 and list the qualities of *agape* love.

_____

_____

Love is patient, love is kind. It does not envy, it does not boast, it is not proud. It is not rude, it is not self-seeking, it is not easily angered, it keeps no record of wrongs. Love does not delight in evil but rejoices with the truth. It always protects, always trusts, always hopes, always perseveres.
1 Corinthians 13:4-7

The word *patient* actually means *a great suffering,* or *enduring suffering.* When we are patient with our husbands, we express a confidence in them to work out their problems or difficulties. When we offer an opinion or advice on every subject, we communicate our lack of confidence. *Kindness* means to be courteous, gracious, and pleasant.

Then Paul lists some qualities that prevent love in our lives. We may not be patient or kind because we are jealous. We may feel our husbands enjoy something in life that we want but do not have, such as a successful career, power, or admiration of others. Envy is a form of covetousness, which is forbidden in the Tenth Commandment (Ex. 20:17).

Often we are not patient or kind because we are anxious to talk about ourselves. We want to boast in our own accomplishments. Perhaps we are proud or rude. Pride stems from a lack of respect for another person or their feelings. One of the major forms of rudeness is sarcasm. We can easily make sarcastic remarks to our husband without considering that these remarks may stem from pride or rudeness.

Love is not self-seeking—stubborn or inflexible, insisting that everyone else adjust to our way of doing things. Love "always protects" or bears all things; literally, it covers everything. When something unpleasant happens, love does not turn around and scatter it all over the neighborhood. Love does not continually bring up the other person's shortcomings. Love covers it or keeps it silent. Ladies, do not spread your husband's mistakes around to others, especially to your mothers, mother-in-laws, or sisters.

Love "always trusts." Love is not gullible, but it is always ready to start over. You are ready to give love another chance. *Agape* love "always hopes." No situation in our marriages and no person is beyond hope. God is the God of miracles. Then Paul says that love "always perseveres." Love never quits; it never gives up on anyone!

What are some practical ways you can demonstrate qualities of *agape* love in your marriage? Be prepared to share your ideas with your group.

_____

_____

_____

First Corinthians 13:8 tells us "love never fails." Unfailing love comes from the Father and is extended to others through the power of the Holy Spirit. If your love often fails, the answer is not to try harder. The answer is prayer and obedience to what God tells you to do. We must love our husbands with *agape* in obedience to our loving heavenly Father.

Paul concludes by affirming the permanence of faith, hope, and love (v. 13). Faith remains because it pleases God (Heb. 11:6). Hope remains because the future is the Lord's and He has prepared a place for us. In time we will know and experience God clearly (1 Cor. 13:12).

Love remains because God is love! God is not faith or hope; He is love. As we learn to love, we will experience more of God because He is love! As you learn to love your husband, you will experience God to a greater degree than ever before! Can you pass up this opportunity? We are taught to follow Christ's example and to live a life of love (Eph. 5:2). Will you make the choice to exemplify *agape* love to your husband? Write your prayer below.

These three remain: faith, hope and love. But the greatest of these is love.
1 Corinthians 13:13

Live a life of love, just as Christ loved us and gave himself up for us as a fragrant offering and sacrifice to God.
Ephesians 5:2

Dear God, _____

_____

_____

Willing Submission

This week you will learn

- the biblical meaning of submission;
- the problem with wanting to be in control;
- the blessing of freedom through submission;
- practical implications of submission;
- misinterpretations regarding submission.

Have you ever met a strong-willed person? Maybe you're thinking, *Yes and it's me!* My parents told me that from birth I was a strong-willed child. My mother blamed a certain child-rearing book for my independent streak, and she refused to use this book with my siblings. I suspect my determination to get my own way can't be blamed on a book; it was just part of my nature.

Recently I heard a speaker refer to my affliction as "the creative child." Well, I was a very creative child, and I have the home movies to prove it. Everything I did was accomplished with determination and commitment—including standing up to my parents on almost every issue.

This strong will did not just automatically disappear when I asked Jesus to come into my life and be my Lord. I was determined to be the best Christian possible. I began distributing tracts to my non-Christian neighbors. Unfortunately, even as a new Christian, I was trying to do the Lord's will in my own power. I never considered asking God what He wanted me to do.

At nine years of age I felt the Lord's call to be a missionary. I told my mother I was going to be a missionary to China. "Why don't you let the Lord tell you where to serve?" she counseled. Would you believe I was still determined to go to China?

My self-confidence, determination, and stubbornness plagued me in the years to come, and I had to learn some hard lessons—especially during the turbulent teen years. You can imagine my dilemma when I learned that as a wife I was to submit to my husband's leadership.

Actually, all believers are told to submit—first to God and then to each other. What exactly then does submission mean for the wife? Does it mean that a wife can never disagree or have a part in decision-making? Does it mean that a wife obeys her husband in the same way a slave obeys his master or a child obeys his parents? Does it mean that a woman's personality is to be repressed or obliterated, having no valid expression?

Probably no other discipline in the Christian faith has been more maligned than submission. My prayer for you this week is that you first submit your life to the lordship of Jesus Christ and then allow God to transform your thinking. One of the mysteries of the Christian life is that we find freedom in obedience. Submission is no exception. God desires to bless your life through an intimate relationship with Him and from obedience to His will.

Day 1
What Is Submission?

Everyone must submit himself to the governing authorities, for there is no authority except that which God has established. Romans 13:1

A good friend of mine in high school and college had a domineering boyfriend. Even though I was still naive about relationships, I sensed that something was wrong with this one. He dictated every decision—even her major. She couldn't go anywhere with me unless she asked his permission. When I tried to talk to her about my concerns, he ordered her not to have anything to do with me.

They got married but eventually divorced. Later my friend told me that her husband's controlling nature broke up their marriage. For years she felt that to be a good wife, she was to submit to him, but, eventually, she couldn't take it any more. Is her experience an example of biblical submission? Is this the picture of Adam and Eve in the garden? Before we explore what the Bible has to say about marital submission, let's define submission.

Submission is an attitude.
The Greek word for submission, *hupotasso*, refers to being willing to rank oneself under or voluntarily yielding. Focus on the words *willing* and *voluntary*. God looks on the heart. He is not impressed by outward acts that don't come from an obedient spirit (I Sam. 16:7).

In the Sermon on the Mount, Jesus taught that the attitudes of the heart were as important as outward acts. The Old Testament law stipulated that we must not murder; Jesus, however, stressed that we murder with our thoughts and words. In a similar way, submission that pleases God comes from the heart. If a wife's heart is full of rebellion, resentment, or rage, outward submission to her husband does not satisfy God's commands.

 Before we continue our discussion of this important topic, place an X on the scale to indicate your attitude about submission.

● ——————————————————————————————————————— ●

I have no desire
to be submissive.

I am unsubmissive
but teachable.

I have a submissive
spirit, including
my relationship
with my husband.

Your honesty at this point is very important to yourself and to God. He knows your thoughts, so there's really no point in dressing up a negative view. At the same time, if you have a positive view of submission, perhaps God has more to teach you on this subject. I have observed women who claimed to believe in the wife's submission yet were known to be the one stubbornly in charge at home. Ladies, submission begins in the spirit. It is an attitude before it can ever be an authentic action.

Submission is God-ordained.

 Read Romans 13:1-2. Underline who Paul said should submit to earthly authority.

Does submitting to those in authority mean that we are not equal in our personhood? (circle)   yes   no

Everyone must submit himself to the governing authorities, for there is no authority except that which God has established. The authorities that exist have been established by God. Consequently, he who rebels against the authority is rebelling against what God has instituted, and those who do so will bring judgment on themselves.
Romans 13:1-2

There is neither Jew nor Greek, slave nor free, male nor female, for you are all one in Christ Jesus.
Galatians 3:28

In Galatians 3:28, Paul said equality in Christ transcends social, ethnic, and sexual differences. Male and female were created equal. Submission, then, is an appeal to one who is equal in personhood to submit to the authority that God has ordained.

 Read I Peter 2:13-17 in the margin on the next page. How does a submissive spirit affect our witness to a lost world?

Our positive attitude toward authority silences our critics! Interestingly, at the time Peter wrote his letter, a godless and brutal emperor named Nero ruled in Rome. We do not submit because we approve of the person in authority. We submit because God ordained authority. Therefore, if submission to human authority is God's will, then rebellion against such authority is actually rebellion against God!

Submission is in our best interests.

Submission to authority provides order in society. In a similar way, submission to each other provides believers with order in the church. In I Corinthians 14:26-40 Paul encourages order during corporate worship.

 How is God described in 1 Corinthians 14:33? _____

God's nature is peace and order. In verses 34-35 Paul addressed the problem of women speaking out during a worship service—not because he was against women speaking publicly (I Cor. 11:5) but because he was concerned about orderly worship.

Rebellion causes problems in all areas of our lives—parenting, marriage, and work. Is it possible that an unsubmissive attitude invites Satan's presence in our lives? Does a lack of submission open us to the possibility of sin? On the other hand, does a submissive spirit help to guard us against the devil's inroads?

 Read James 4:7. How is submitting to God a way to resist

Satan? _____

When we have unsubmissive spirits, we must identify the real enemy. It's not our husbands, bosses, or coworkers, but Satan himself. His desire is to sow discord in all our relationships. We are promised that if we submit to God and resist the devil, then Satan will flee from us. That awesome formula gives us the proper perspective. We are first to humble ourselves before God and then to resist Satan's subtle temptations.

Not only does a submissive spirit help protect us from Satanic attack, but also it frees us to do good. A helpful illustration is obeying the speed limit. If we are speeding, we find ourselves looking around for a policeman or speed camera. When we drive the speed limit, we are free to concentrate on driving without worry and fear. God desires that we live a

Submit yourselves for the Lord's sake to every authority instituted among men: whether to the king, as the supreme authority, or to governors, who are sent by him to punish those who do wrong and to commend those who do right. For it is God's will that by doing good you should silence the ignorant talk of foolish men. Live as free men, but do not use your freedom as a cover-up for evil; live as servants of God. Show proper respect to everyone: Love the brotherhood of believers, fear God, honor the king.
1 Peter 2:13-17

God is not a God of disorder but of peace.
1 Corinthians 14:33

Submit yourselves, then, to God. Resist the devil, and he will flee from you.
James 4:7

life of freedom, and submission is an avenue to this freedom. When we submit willingly and freely to God, we know Who is in control. Satan no longer can hold on to us through worry and fear. However, we do not submit simply out of self-interest; we submit because we want to please God in all that we do.

Submission is...

• an attitude.

• God ordained.

• in our best interest.

• a decision.

Submission is a decision.

Submission is not mindless or childlike obedience without responsibility for one's actions. If God's rules conflict with earthly rules, a believer must choose to obey God. If your boss asks you to lie about something, you are to obey, instead, what God has directed you to do. Sometimes we may be called on to suffer because we are submissive to God's will. Peter tells us that if we suffer for doing good, God is pleased with us (see 1 Peter 2:19).

Recall from page 53 that when we define submission, we are to focus on the words *willing* and *voluntary*. Submission to earthly authorities is a choice. We can choose to disobey the laws and receive the punishment. Likewise, submission to our husbands is a choice. We can insist on having our way and being in charge. However, when we do not follow God's blueprint for marriage, we cannot in good faith ask for His blessings on our family.

We have three choices. **First,** we can simply refuse to submit to anyone—including our husbands. **Second,** we may simply submit outwardly but with a heart of rebellion. **Third,** we can submit from the heart in order to please the Lord our God. What is your response today? Will you pray that God will give you a desire to be submissive to Him first, and then to His authorities here on earth?

Dear God, _____

_____

_____

Day 2

Who Is in Control?

The wisdom that comes from heaven is . . . submissive. James 3:17

In the introduction to week 3, I shared with you that I was a creative child—I tried to create an environment in which I controlled everyone and everything. I thank the Lord that my parents weren't willing to let me have my own way. However, their resolve led to many confrontations.

As a teenager, I rebelled against all authority including my parents. Fortunately, I had a life-changing experience with the Lord, and my attitudes began to change. The Lord confronted me about my will. I realized that my rebellion wasn't really against my parents or society but against God Himself. This awareness was the first of many changes that God needed to make in my life.

When I got married, God continued the process of change. I was determined to marry a good Christian man, and I did. I was just as determined that he conform to my expectations. Imagine my surprise when he had a mind of his own! Needless to say, I had some rough lessons to learn.

Recall from week 1 that marriage was designed to enrich our lives, but when sin takes charge, it can literally paralyze the love relationship. Sin is the root problem, manifested as selfishness or wanting control over our environment and others.

Submission is a longing after God and a willingness to allow Him to have control of everything. It's not achieved by willpower or determination but comes moment by moment as we allow the Lord to direct us. We develop the discipline of submission when we willingly place all of our desires, wants, and dreams before God, who is then free to give us the desires of our heart.

Is your marriage a battle zone?

The opposite of submission is rebellion or wanting to get your own way. When our whole focus is controlling our environment and all the people in it, we are putting our will before the Lord's. What is the result? We fight and quarrel to get what we want. Marriage becomes a battleground to see who is going to be in control.

What causes fights and quarrels among you? Don't they come from your desires that battle within you? You want something but don't get it. You kill and covet, but you cannot have what you want. You quarrel and fight. You do not have, because you do not ask God.
James 4:1-2

James clearly identified the problem. Read James 4:1-2. What causes

fights and quarrels? _____

The need to control is the real issue in conflict. Do you know people who are so obsessed with things going the way they planned that all joy and happiness are squelched? People will spend days, weeks, and even years obsessing about some little thing that did not go as they wished. Their resentment makes them and everyone around them miserable.

In the following list of issues over which husbands and wives fight for control, check those that have been battlegrounds in your marriage.

☐ **Power.** In study after study, finances is the number one reason given for divorce. Money is not the real problem; it is only a symbol of power. According to the world, whoever controls the money controls the power.

☐ **Position.** One of the world's myths is that in order to be a person of worth, we must have the top position with others beneath us. In an adult version of king of the mountain, husbands and wives are often determined to be the one on top. That means pushing the other one down.

☐ **Pleasure.** The world also tells us that we have the right to be happy even if it is at someone else's expense. Happiness is a greater virtue than sacrifice or service. Many feel their right to have possessions, recreation, or leisure should win out—even if others have to do without.

☐ **Pride.** Pride is a symptom of either low self-esteem or an exalted opinion of self. Pride is basically selfishness. Pride measures everyone else through the lens of self. The desire to look good to others or to be right may exceed the desire for truth, understanding, or communication.

Perhaps you only checked one of the four, but surely all of us at one time or another have felt our marriages were a war zone. In some cases, a secret war was being waged, and those fighting didn't even know they were at war. For example, wives nag, withhold sex, or quietly pout and withdraw—all to get their own way. Husbands may try passive aggression—such as never getting around to those household projects. Have you ever had the silent treatment used against you?

Then there are the more outward conflicts: yelling, name-calling, hitting, threatening, or even causing destruction. This overt war is unpredictable and may become a way of life for two unhappy people.

 Describe your marriage at this time. Underline one or more.

Civil war   dictatorship   peace   temporary peace

anarchy   negotiated settlement   World War III

How can you become a peacemaker?

What is the biblical solution for power struggles in marriage? The book of James points us to behaviors and attitudes that can end them.

Seek wisdom from God (James 1:5).

James says that true wisdom from above can direct us to the kind of behaviors and attitudes that stop this need to control. The outstanding characteristic of this wisdom is humility.

 Read James 1:5. How can we have this wisdom from God?

_____

God does not just offer instant wisdom. When James said, "it will be given to him," he used the verb that means that we don't just receive this wisdom once, but it comes in a steady flow as we need it. This wisdom results from daily time spent with the Lord.

 Read James 3:14-17. Circle the words below that describe God's wisdom.

peaceloving   envious   submissive   selfishly ambitious

disorderly   prideful   considerate

Many of us pray for wisdom, but we don't pray for the Lord to make us more submissive in our spirits. If we are not willing to cultivate submissive spirits, we need not pray for God's wisdom.

If any of you lacks wisdom, he should ask God, who gives generously to all without finding fault, and it will be given to him.
James 1:5

If you harbor bitter envy and selfish ambition in your hearts, do not boast about it or deny the truth. Such "wisdom" does not come down from heaven but is earthly, unspiritual, of the devil. For where you have envy and selfish ambition, there you find disorder and every evil practice.

But the wisdom that comes from heaven is first of all pure; then peaceloving, considerate, submissive, full of mercy and good fruit, impartial and sincere.
James 3:14-17

Humble yourself before God (James 4:10).

The opposite of humility is living life as if God does not exist. Many call on God as though He were a divine emergency system. Such a view of God is arrogant and presumptuous; He desires a relationship with us.

Humble yourselves before the Lord, and he will lift you up.
James 4:10

 Read James 4:10. Underline what happens when we come humbly before God.

Trust God with tomorrow (James 4:13-16).

When we submit our will to God, we are acknowledging our limited understanding and inability to control our lives. We don't even know what is going to happen tomorrow, but God's will is all-knowing. Freedom comes from seeing that our plans are not our own, our time is not our own, and our lives do not even belong to us; then we are free to place our dependence on God.

Now listen, you who say, "Today or tomorrow we will go to this or that city, spend a year there, carry on business and make money." Why, you do not even know what will happen tomorrow. What is your life? You are a mist that appears for a little while and then vanishes. Instead, you ought to say, "If it is the Lord's will, we will live and do this or that." As it is, you boast and brag. All such boasting is evil. Anyone, then, who knows the good he ought to do and doesn't do it, sins.
James 4:13-16

 Read James 4:13-16. Underline what we should say as we make plans for tomorrow.

Draw near to God daily (James 4:8).

We need to be in an continual state of fellowship with the Lord. I don't know about you, but if as I rise from bed in the morning, I say, "Lord this day belongs to You, do with me whatever is Your will," the day goes much better. A day that is not begun with the Lord probably will not end with the Lord.

Lack of submission is a terrible burden—even if we succeed in controlling others. We can be a slave to Christ or a slave to our sinful natures; there is no third choice (Rom. 6:16). When we draw near to the Lord, we are giving up our right to have our way and acknowledging that we want God to have His way in our lives. Today, thank Jesus for paying the price to be your Savior.

Dear God, _____

_____

_____

Day 3

Freedom Through Submission

Wives, submit to your husbands as to the Lord. Ephesians 5:22

When I got married, I had Ephesians 5:22 included in my wedding vows. I was going on record that I was willing to be submissive to my husband. A friend whose wedding was a month after my wedding heard my vows. She exclaimed, "No way am I going to put that verse in my vows!" She probably had more of a handle on what those verses really were saying than I did. As I have explained, I had a lot to learn about God's design for marriage.

Although many women think of submission in marriage as bondage, it can be a source of freedom. No longer are you consumed with getting your own way. Because you are free to focus on God and His will, you can take your eyes off of yourself and see the needs of others around you. When your acceptance comes from God, you are able to love without demanding love in return.

When applied to marriage, an other-focus allows your husband's dreams and plans to become important to you. You can love unconditionally because you have experienced God's love for you.

A Child of the Light

Paul wrote Ephesians 4:17-19 to the Christians at Ephesus, exhorting them to live as children of the light. In order to make his point clear, he began by describing children of darkness.

 Read Ephesians 4:17-32 in your Bible. Under each heading below, write several characteristics describing these two types of individuals.

children of the light	children of the darkness

Paul describes the old self in verse 22 as "corrupted by its deceitful desires." When our focus is on satisfying all our desires, this old line of thinking does not lead us to the light of Christ.

Live in the light.

After Paul describes the life that we are to live, he concludes, "For you were once darkness, but now you are light in the Lord. Live as children of light" (Eph. 5:8).

Put on the new self, created to be like God in true righteousness and holiness.
Ephesians 4:24

 What is the first step in freedom living according to Ephesians 4:24?

_____

Freedom living is living like God in true righteousness and holiness. Paul repeats this theme in Ephesians 5:1-2. "Be imitators of God ... and live a life of love, just as Christ loved us and gave himself up for us as a fragrant offering and sacrifice to God." How do we know the life God has for us? Paul says, "find out what pleases the Lord" (Eph. 5:10). In other words, God is very eager to show us how we are to live. We cannot say that we do not know His desires for us, because He has made His will very clear in His Word.

Paul concludes, "Be very careful, then, how you live—not as unwise but as wise" (5:15). In day 2 we discussed the characteristics of God's wisdom. Can you recall one or more of these? Review page 59 to remind yourself of the path of godly wisdom.

Submit to each other.

Out of the context of living a life of wisdom as an imitator of God, Paul writes, "Submit to one another out of reverence for Christ" (Eph. 5:21).

 Who is Paul speaking to in verse 21? (check one)
- ☐ all believers
- ☐ women
- ☐ wives only

In the preceding verses, Paul indicates two criteria that enable believers to be submissive.

1. Be filled with God's Spirit (Eph. 5:18).

Submission is possible because believers are filled with God's Spirit. Remember that a characteristic of non-Christians is a spirit of deceitful desires (Eph. 4:22).

The motivation for our submission is the fear, or reverence, we have for Christ (Eph. 5:21). This word *fear* in Greek is *phobos* and literally means to show deference to, to feel respect for or reverential fear. We submit because our main priority is to please God in all we say and do.

2. Give thanks to God for everything (Eph. 5:19-20).

A grateful heart remembers all that God has done for us in Christ. Our gratitude expresses itself by joyful music in our hearts. We have a new nature only because of what Christ did for us on the cross. Because He is Lord, we live in faithful obedience to Him. In the following verses Paul describes different situations in which we are to submit: wives to husbands, children to parents, and slaves to their masters.

Submit to your husbands.

Do you recall from day 1 the meaning of the word *submit?* (See page 53.) Wives are to be submissive *(hupotasso)*, which shows a willingness to yield to their own husbands in love. Notice that they are not to be submissive to all men but to their own husbands.

Wives are to submit "as to the Lord." This expression is also found in Colossians 3:18: "Wives, submit to your husbands, as is fitting in the Lord." Does this mean that somehow your husband becomes the Lord in your eyes? Should you submit to him unquestioningly just as if he were God? No. This Scripture means that you submit to your husband's leadership as an act of obedience to the Lord. You show your obedience to Christ by how you submit to your husband.

> You show your obedience to Christ by how you submit to your husband.

The word *fitting* in Colossians 3:18 is *aneko* and means well fitted, well placed and ready for use. Wives should be vessels ready for the Lord to use. Focus on God rather than on yourself. Have a readiness of the heart, not just of outward obedience.

This submission is an attitude which characterizes the wife's response to her husband. It's not a mechanical response of obedience. A woman can be completely honest, straightforward, and even confrontational with her husband and still be submissive. Look to your attitude within. As a wife, does your heart truly want the best for your husband? Are you supportive and encouraging to your husband?

This submission has nothing to do with inferiority. In fact, Jesus was submissive to God the Father's will, even to the point of death. In Scripture the Spirit submits to the Son (John 16:12-15). There is no inferiority implied, just order. In Ephesians 5:23 we read, "The husband is the head of the wife as Christ is the head of the church, his body, of which he is the Savior." This verse is one of the most difficult and controversial passages in the Bible.

I want you to realize that the head of every man is Christ, and the head of the woman is man, and the head of Christ is God.
1 Corinthians 11:3

Read I Corinthians 11:3 and list the order of authority given.

The authority over every man is _____.

The authority over woman is _____.

The authority over Christ is_____.

Paul said that Christ is the authority over every man, man is the authority over woman, and God is the authority over Christ. If we follow this analogy, the Son is not inferior to the Father. Rather, the Son willingly submits Himself to the Father's authority. They have a different function, but They are equal in essence and worth.

Women are equal to men in their personhood, yet they have a different role in the home. These differences don't logically imply inequality or inferiority, just as Christ's submission to God does not imply inferiority.

As the church submits to Christ, so also wives should submit to their husbands in everything.
Ephesians 5:24

Read Ephesians 5:24.

Wives are to be subject to their husbands in what? _____

Who is our example in this submission? _____

The word *everything* includes our attitudes and actions—an inward desiring of God's will. Many blessings result from biblical submission. When I finally was able to turn my will over to the Lord and truly be submissive in my heart to my husband, there was indescribable freedom! I was finally free to enjoy meeting someone else's needs, rather than being in bondage to my own selfish desires.

Today will you follow Christ's example and turn over the control of your life to Him? Rest in the freedom God has for you.

Day 4

Submission in Practice

However, each one of you also must love his wife as he loves himself, and the wife must respect her husband. Ephesians 5:33

Today we will deal with some of the practical issues of submission, including the husband's role in this process. Then we will examine what God has to say to the wife of an unbeliever.

The Husband's Role

Christ is the example for both husband and wife in the biblical blueprint for marriage.

 Read Ephesians 5:25-33. Paul instructed husbands (check one)

☐ to dominate their wives in order to get their own way.
☐ to love their wives sacrificially as Christ loved the church.

Paul takes three verses to address wives and then nine verses to address husbands. In Paul's day, wives were considered personal property. Men could divorce their wives for virtually any reason. Since women were not allowed to own property or work away from home, they were financially dependent on their husband or sons. Devout Hebrew men began their day by thanking God that they were not Gentiles, slaves, or women.

Paul calls on husbands to live in the light of the cross, to build a different kind of marriage based on Christ's role model. Paul directed a husband to sacrificially love *(agape)* his wife just as Christ loved and died for the church (Eph. 5: 25,28-29). His wife was to be more important than his parents. He was to encourage, build up, and help his wife to be all that God intended for her. Because of his loving leadership, she would grow in beauty, wholeness, purity, and godliness.

Verse 32 explains why the marriage relationship is so important to our witness to the world: "This is a profound mystery—but I am talking about Christ and the church." Our marriages are a picture to the world of Christ and the relationship He has with His people!

Although we may think our submission to our husbands is the harder cross to bear, consider what Paul asked husbands to do. Husbands were

Husbands, love your wives, just as Christ loved the church and gave himself up for her to make her holy, cleansing her by the washing with water through the word, and to present her to himself as a radiant church, without stain or wrinkle or any other blemish, but holy and blameless. In this same way, husbands ought to love their wives as their own bodies. He who loves his wife loves himself. After all, no one ever hated his own body, but he feeds and cares for it, just as Christ does the church—for we are members of his body. "For this reason a man will leave his father and mother and be united to his wife, and the two will become one flesh." This is a profound mystery—but I am talking about Christ and the church. However, each one of you also must love his wife as he loves himself, and the wife must respect her husband. Ephesians 5:25-33

65

to sacrifice for their wives, even to the point of death. Christ's ultimate submission to the Father was His death on the cross for our sins. In the garden, Christ prayed, "Not my will, but thine" (Luke 22:42, KJV). These were not easy words to pray. As wives, we must ask ourselves, *Do I love my husband enough to live for him?* Husbands must ask themselves, *Do I love my wife enough to die for her?*

What are some examples of a husband's sacrificial love for his wife?

_____

_____

Wives find it much easier to submit to a husband who sacrificially loves his wife in the same way he loves his own body. Do you see God's grand design—husbands and wives in an unending cycle of sacrificial love and willing submission? When either party does not function according to God's design, the marriage suffers.

Husbands, in the same way be considerate as you live with your wives, and treat them with respect as the weaker partner and as heirs with you of the gracious gift of life, so that nothing will hinder your prayers.
1 Peter 3:7

Paraphrase the instructions Peter gives husbands in 1 Peter 3:7.

_____

_____

Recall from page 14 that wives are vessels of honor, fine china if you will. Peter said to the husbands that if they didn't treat their wives properly, their prayers would be hindered. Being harsh, bitter, demanding, and arrogant will result in unanswered prayers. God is a just God, and He cares for those who are in vulnerable positions.

The Wife's Role

I wonder how many of our prayers are unanswered because of an unwillingness to be submissive to God and to our husbands. We must examine our own hearts and see if there are any wrong motives or attitudes.

Read 1 Peter 3:5-6 on the next page. Underline whom Peter called an example of submission.

I am so glad that Sarah was used as a model of submission, for she was far from perfect. I would have found it more difficult to relate to Ruth, whose mistakes and misjudgments are not recorded in the Bible. Sarah was strong-willed and made mistakes, yet Sarah was given to us as an example of submission. Sarah submitted to Abraham in following him where God led, which was an act of faith on both of their parts.

Sarah gave her husband advice (Gen. 16:1-6).

Abraham often heeded Sarah's advice. Sarah was not silent about her decisions, and she was actively involved in running Abraham's household. Of course, Sarah was also wrong on occasion! Sarah had the misguided idea for Abraham to conceive a son by Hagar. Sarah reminds us that our opinions are just as fallible as our husbands' may be on occasion. We must never arrogantly assume we always have the best idea. However, God assured Abraham that he should listen to his wife's advice about sending away Hagar and Ishmael (Gen. 21:12).

Sarah protected her husband (Gen. 12:10-13; 20:1-7).

Remember what happened to Sarah when Abraham abandoned her twice to kings' harems? Even though she went along with Abraham's dishonest schemes, God rescued her in both situations! God will also take care of you, sometimes by removing you from the situation and often by giving you strength in the situation.

Sarah had a strong personality (Gen. 21:9-13).

She was no doormat! When Hagar became pregnant and began taunting her mistress, Sarah "dealt harshly with her" (Gen. 16:6, NKJV). After giving Hagar a second chance, she finally told Abraham to send her away for good (21:10).

Sarah learned to trust God (Gen. 17:15-17; 18:9-15).

God honored Sarah's life and blessed her with being the "mother of nations" (Gen. 17: 16). Like her husband, who laughed at the news of an offspring (v. 17), Sarah had to learn to trust God, even when she had doubts about His will for her. Our submission is to God first and then to our husbands.

How are you like Sarah? _____

This is the way the holy women of the past who put their hope in God used to make themselves beautiful. They were submissive to their own husbands, like Sarah, who obeyed Abraham and called him her master. You are her daughters if you do what is right and do not give way to fear.
1 Peter 3:5-6

🏺 How does the story of her life encourage you? _____

_____

To this you were called,
because Christ suffered
for you, leaving you an
example, that you should
follow his steps.
"He committed no sin,
*   and no deceit was found*
*   in his mouth."*
When they hurled their
insults at him, he did not
retaliate; when he suffered,
he made no threats. Instead,
he entrusted himself to him
who judges justly. He
himself bore our sins in his
body on the tree, so that we
might die to sins and live
for righteousness; by his
wounds you have been
healed. For you were like
sheep going astray, but now
you have returned to the
Shepherd and Overseer of
your souls.

Wives, in the same way
be submissive to your
husbands so that, if any
of them do not believe the
word, they may be won
over without words by the
behavior of their wives.
1 Peter 2:21–3:2

Acknowledge that you don't always need the last word.
Sarah had reverent respect for her husband (I Pet. 3:6). The need to be in control and always to be right stand in the way of godly submission for many wives. If you are caught in the sinful pattern of self-righteousness, ask God to humble you. Pride becomes a formidable barrier to knowing God. Don't let it keep you from Him.

If Your Husband Is an Unbeliever

Christ is our example for both husband and wife in biblical submission. What if your husband is not a Christian? Are you then freed from the command to submit to him?

🏺 Read I Peter 2: 21–3:2. To whom does Peter compare a wife's

submission? _____

What hope does Peter give wives of unbelievers? _____

_____

Peter calls on wives to respond with the same spirit of submission that characterized Christ. Just as Christ entrusted His life to His Father in heaven, a wife must entrust hers to God within the marriage.

If a woman decides to marry a non-Christian, this passage does not guarantee her good conduct will win her husband to Christ. God's Word clearly says that a Christian should marry only another Christian (I Cor. 7:39; 2 Cor. 6:14). In the case of the women to whom Peter wrote, the wives had come to Christ after they were married. Unfortunately, their husbands had not yet become Christians.

Peter offered wives the hope that no matter what their situations, they could trust the Lord. Perhaps you may be thinking, *But what about my situation? God surely has another plan for me.* Our heavenly Father knows our strengths as well as our weaknesses; He also sees when there is injustice and inequity. He knows our hearts and motives, and we can freely commit ourselves to a just God.

The behavior (Greek, *anastrophe*) of the wife in I Peter 3:1 refers to her manner of life. This behavior was not just a one-time kindness, but a Spirit-filled life. This woman transferred her hopes and dreams from her husband to the Lord where they belonged. She was then free to approach her husband with gentleness, meekness, and full submission.

You can submit to your husband because you know that you are the vessel God can use to pour His life into the life of your husband. Will you pray a prayer of willingness to the Lord? If you are married to a believer, pray for someone who is not married to a believer.

Dear God, _____

_____

_____

Day 5
Misconceptions

Whatever you do, whether in word or deed, do it all in the name of the Lord Jesus.
Colossians 3:17

This week we have learned that God wants submission to flow from our hearts. Our submission to our husbands indicates our submission to God. Unfortunately, because sin entered into the perfect plan that God created, the principle of submission can be misused.

Sometimes wives don't live up to God's standards for our marriages, and sometimes husbands fail to follow God's model. Submission is never easy, even under the best of circumstances, but today we want to look at a woman's submission when she isn't married to Prince Charming—when she does not have an ideal relationship with her husband. What does the Bible say about being married to a husband who is a Christian but just difficult to live with? What about abusive situations? For many of these situations, we will not find an exact verse to follow, but we can find principles which give us guidelines.

None of us lives to himself alone and none of us dies to himself alone. If we live, we live to the Lord; and if we die, we die to the Lord. So, whether we live or die, we belong to the Lord.

For this very reason, Christ died and returned to life so that he might be the Lord of both the dead and the living. You, then, why do you judge your brother? Or why do you look down on your brother? For we will all stand before God's judgment seat. It is written:
" 'As surely as I live,'
*   says the Lord,*
'every knee will bow
*   before me;*
*   every tongue will confess*
*   to God.' "*
So then, each of us will give an account of himself to God.
Romans 14:7-12

Guidelines for Submission

Submission to God takes priority.

Read Romans 14:7-12. Paul's ultimate goal was God's approval rather than the temporal rewards of praise and acknowledgment on earth. As he looked back at his life, he realized that he was accountable to only one Person—God Himself.

Paul realized God's opinion was the most important to cultivate. Memorize Romans 14:7-8. When times are tough and you feel you don't please your husband or others, recall these verses. Focus on what God thinks of you. God's praises are eternal.

Submission to God precedes submission to governing authorities.

In the following examples, underline who did not submit and why.

1. The Egyptian midwives did not submit to the government when ordered to kill all the boy babies. Moses' life was saved by this action (Ex. 1:15-2:4).
2. Rahab hid the Hebrew spies. She and her family were spared when Jericho was destroyed (Josh. 2:1-21; 6:22-23).
3. Daniel's friends refused to bow to the king's golden image. They trusted God to rescue them from the fiery furnace (Dan. 3:16-18).
4. Because they obeyed God rather than men, Peter and John refused to stop preaching in the name of Jesus (Acts 4:18-22).

Submission to God precedes submission to husbands.

Read I Samuel 25:2-38 in your Bible. How did Abigail refuse

to support her husband's foolish instructions? _____

_____

Abigail did not support Nabal's refusal to show hospitality to David and his men because he put his life and the lives of those working for him in danger. Her motive was to protect him and to do him good.

A negative example of a woman who supported her husband's actions is found in the story of Ananias and Sapphira in Acts 5:1-11. Because Sapphira cooperated with her husband's dishonesty, she lost her life. Clearly, human authority can be abused. As children of God, we must obey our Father. We are never free to sin because our husbands ask us to disobey God. This is a misinterpretation of submission.

Submission does not justify abuse.

Another misinterpretation involves the belief that a woman must put up with an abusive situation because marriage is a lifelong commitment. No biblical support exists for the abuse of women and children. To use verses on marital submission as justification for such actions is heresy. In some marriages, the time may come when a wife may need to say, "enough is enough"!

> **Finding Help**
> Ask your pastor or another church staff member for a list of Christian counselors in your area.

Abuse can be subtle. One type of abuse is intimidation. A wife may live each day walking on pins and needles afraid she will do something to displease her husband. Another type of abuse is humiliation, being insulted regularly with a resulting loss of self-esteem.

Some women are deprived of essential items, or their husbands control every penny they spend. Others are isolated, kept away from other people or unable to do anything without permission.

Are you in an abusive situation? Let me encourage you to seek godly counseling. Don't delay! Get informed biblical advice when determining if you or someone you love is in an abusive situation. Abuse cannot be taken lightly. Here are some principles to follow if you are in an abusive situation.

1. Bring the abuse out into the open. The worst thing you can do is keep the abuse a secret. This action essentially gives permission for the abuse to continue. Abusers do not want exposure, and they will use manipulation to keep their wives quiet. Talk to godly advisors, share your problems, and get feedback.

2. Abuse is a compulsive behavior. The situation will not necessarily get better without intensive counseling and commitment to change.

3. Many women who find themselves in an abusive relationship have been led to believe it's their fault. A common statement by an abuser is, "You made me do it." Let me assure you, you are not responsible for another person's actions.

4. Some women have been taught that if you are in a difficult situation, just sit still and pray. Pray, of course, but also seek godly advice.

5. Reconciliation is the goal; however, this goal does not mean you stay in a house where your life (emotionally and physically) may be in danger. If separation is needed for a time, hopefully your husband will recognize his need for help and get serious counseling. I have known situations where strong marriages resulted from this approach.

6. Women often get locked into abusive situations for financial reasons. They think if they take their children and leave, they will have no financial resources. God is in the business of taking care of His children, and He cares about your finances. God may provide for you through a shelter for women and children; if so, consider that God's provision for this time in your life.

A lady told me that she would consider herself very selfish if she put her interests above her husband's, and she stayed in an impossible situation. Jesus gave as the second greatest commandment, "Love your neighbor as yourself" (Mark 12:31). Caring for yourself recognizes your value to the Creator. In turn, care for others in the same way you care for yourself.

God will not leave your side. He will give you the strength you need for whatever you have to bear. God will give you the wisdom to make the decisions that you need to make. He will provide people to counsel with you. Ultimately, He will bring you to safety in His heavenly kingdom.

Write Philippians 4:19 in the space provided.

_____

_____

God is waiting to give you the courage and the strength for whatever decision needs to be made today! Write out a prayer below.

Dear God, _____

_____

_____

Week Four

Virtuous Character

Have you ever groaned when you heard someone mention the virtuous woman of Proverbs 31? She was such a model wife and mother, with a smoothly running household and a loving family who adored her. At times in my life, all I needed to send me over the edge was to be compared with her! Have you been there?

I recall such a time in my life. After sserving as missionaries in the Philippines for eight years, my family found ourselves in the United States again. Our task was to begin a new church in our home. At the same time, I was working full time in a counseling ministry where I was on call at odd hours. I found it difficult to leave the problems at the clinic. After a busy day of work, I would often come home to a house full of people who were involved in a meeting—and three hungry children.

One particular day I came home from work just in time to lead our Wednesday prayer meeting. The group was sharing prayer requests when I felt a tap on my shoulder. I turned around and motioned for my son, Matthew, to wait until we finished sharing, but he was persistent. Finally I asked him, "Matt, what is it?" Matt replied, "I was blowing my nose when ..." Just then smoke came billowing down the hallway of our house. Everyone screamed, the fire alarm went off, and I ran toward the source of the smoke. I found the trash can in the bathroom on fire!

After the fire was extinguished and our nerves had calmed, I asked Matthew to explain what had happened. He repeated, "I was blowing my nose ..." You see, he had been watching himself blow his nose in the bathroom mirror while leaning over a scented candle. The tissue caught on fire, so he threw it into a basket of potpourri which then caught on fire! Not knowing what to do, he threw the potpourri basket into the trash can—hence the fire!

This week you will learn to

- identify the qualities of godly women;
- identify your stage of life;
- understand your role as the manager of your home;
- balance work both inside and outside of your home;
- value ministry to others outside of your home.

Have you experienced a day like this? Have you had someone tell you this is a character building experience? Have you ever felt like saying, "I can't handle any more character"?

As you approach this week's study, may I suggest that Proverbs 31 can bring balance to your life. When you know your priorities and God's plan for you, you can better manage your household. That may not keep your son from blowing his nose over a candle, but God's peace and perspective on how to look at the situation will reign.

Day 1

The Proverbs 31 Woman

A wife of noble character who can find? She is worth far more than rubies.
Proverbs 31:10

At this writing I have two children in college and one teenager at home. The pulls on me have increased rather than decreased, but God has been faithful! He has miraculously put balance in my life despite the odds. Even through consistent chaos in my life, God gives me peace! Rather than worrying and being tense about my precious children, God grows my faith to trust in Him. Allow me to share with you how God used the Proverbs 31 woman to encourage my spiritual journey.

Read in your Bible Proverbs 31:10-31 completely and slowly. Make notes in the margin about verses that have special meaning to you.

Does anything in this passage bother you? (circle) yes no

Possibly this passage makes you angry because it seems to set you up for failure. You may feel depressed or even hopeless. Recent words you have spoken to your husband and children may keep echoing in your thoughts. Missed opportunities or careless actions may ricochet through your mind.

Perhaps you are thinking about spurned attempts to be this type of woman. Perhaps you have had your good intentions thrown back in your face. You may feel unappreciated or even unloved. What should you do with these feelings? The first step is to admit to yourself and to God (who already knows) what you are feeling. This step can be very painful. Next, tell Him you are open to insights from this passage that will continue the good work He has begun in you (see Phil. 1:6).

She is a role model.

King Lemuel's mother wrote this poem to him to explain what type of wife he should seek (Prov. 31:1). Knowing that a mother wrote this passage gives me an automatic identification. In my eyes my sons are also kings, and I definitely want the right type of wife for them. Also, I know that children learn much more from example and nonverbal behavior than from words. Not only do I need to be a good wife for my husband, but I need to model for my sons what type of wife they should seek. I am also modeling the role of wife for my daughter.

List one way your mother modeled the role of wife. _____

_____

Was this a good model? Why or why not? _____

_____

List one way you seek to model the role of a godly wife. _____

_____

King Lemuel's mother drilled him repeatedly on the character traits of this model wife. The dictionary defines *model* as *a small image of the real thing.* When I am tempted to give up my pursuit of character, I remind myself that I can at least be a small image of the real thing. God has worked in my life by making one change at a time. He doesn't expect us to approach Him only when we have it all together. God will make the changes He desires by His gentle hand, and they are for our good. Whether you feel you are a model wife or far from it, begin where you are.

Whether you feel you are a model wife or far from it, begin where you are.

She has virtuous character.

The poem begins with an introductory statement: "An excellent wife, who can find? For her worth is far above jewels" (v. 10, NASB). The adjective *excellent* refers to strong, moral, virtuous, and noble character. In the Bible this word portrays men who are dynamic and valiant. In this context, it speaks of a woman's strength of character. The model wife is a precious gem, increasing in value with age, her character continually developing along with her abilities.

Why is this type of wife so difficult to find? Check one or more.
- [ ] Our culture doesn't value character.
- [ ] We want a quick fix, a make-over.
- [ ] We concentrate on outward appearance.
- [ ] Character requires discipline and sacrifice.

Character describes who we are inside, the real you and me. It refers to an enduring state, not a temporary emotion or action. We become persons of excellent character over time. Like gems which have to be chiseled and polished to reveal their true value, we are God's workmanship. He is chiseling and shaping us into the persons He has called us to be. Paul said, "we do not lose heart. Though outwardly we are wasting away, yet inwardly we are being renewed day by day" (2 Cor. 4:16).

God has a plan for your life. By allowing Him to make one change at a time, He can chisel you into that precious gem that only grows more valuable with time.

Read Jeremiah 29:11. Write God's plan for you. _____

_____

She is trustworthy.

Read Proverbs 31:11-12. Why would the husband of the excellent

wife trust her? _____

Her husband trusted her character because she was a woman of virtue. I can't overemphasize the importance of cultivating godly character. The word *integrity* comes from *integer*, or *one*. A whole person, fully integrated in heart, soul, mind, and strength has transparent motives and actions— not double meanings, manipulation, or evil intent.

"I know the plans I have for you," declares the Lord, "plans to prosper you and not to harm you, plans to give you hope and a future."
Jeremiah 29:11

The heart of her husband trusts in her, And he will have no lack of gain. She does him good and not evil all the days of her life.
Proverbs 31:11-12, NASB

Read these verses and list positive outcomes of being a virtuous wife.

Proverbs 12:4 _____

Proverbs 18:22 _____

Proverbs 19:14 _____

*A wife of noble character is
her husband's crown,
but a disgraceful wife is
like decay in his bones.*
Proverbs 12:4

The virtuous woman's husband trusted her with their assets, knowing
that whatever she did was for his good.

*He who finds a wife finds
what is good
and receives favor from
the Lord.*
Proverbs 18:22

Check the following ways that build your husband's trust in you.
- [ ] checking with him before you make a major purchase
- [ ] keeping your checkbook up-to-date or receipts filed
- [ ] telling him about purchases (never hiding them!)
- [ ] living within an agreed-upon budget
- [ ] refusing to use money as a weapon to punish or retaliate

*Houses and wealth are
inherited from parents,
but a prudent wife is
from the Lord.*
Proverbs 19:14

Remember that your role as a suitable helper is to protect your husband's
heart. When we are deceitful or manipulative, we tear away layers of
trust. Trust—a very fragile quality—is essential to an intimate marriage.
Trust is easily lost and difficult to earn back. Words we have spoken in
front of our husbands and to others about our husbands can be very
damaging. Will you ask the Lord to bring to mind anything that you
have said or done that showed you to be untrustworthy? Confess these to
the Lord and to your husband, and start the healing process.

Does your husband have full confidence in you? (circle)   yes   no

What can you do to become more trustworthy? _____

She is committed.

Verse 12 refers to the wife's commitment to her husband. Underline
how long she was to remain in the relationship.

*She brings him good,
not harm,
all the days of her life.*
Proverbs 31:12

The Proverbs 31 Woman is...
- a role model.
- trustworthy.
- committed.

The Proverbs 31 woman was committed to her husband's welfare as long as she lived. Her commitment did not waver. Security in a relationship is another way we build trust with our husbands.

Building noble character is a process through which God molds us and creates us into precious gems. Write a prayer asking God to bless, strengthen, and encourage you in what is right and good!

> *Dear God,* _____
>
> _____
>
> _____

Day 2

Stages of an Excellent Wife

She . . . works with eager hands. Proverbs 31:13

Proverbs 31:10-31 is an acrostic poem which shows how this capable woman demonstrated excellence as a wife and mother. I think of it as a progression through the stages of her life. It's not a snapshot but rather a video, showing her total life. She didn't accomplish everything mentioned in these verses every day, month, or year. Now, don't you feel better?

The more I read and meditate on Proverbs 31, the more I realize that this passage was not written to encourage my already over-developed tendency to busyness! Rather, it reminds me of the vast scope of interests and activities that are open to me as a woman. Although many opportunities were available to women three thousand years ago, many more exciting challenges and opportunities are available to us today! God is pleased when we become everything He has equipped us to be.

Some activities are easier at one stage than another. For example, I look forward to the day when my children are grown, and I can get more involved in teaching and full-time ministry. But right now, I love this very short time when they are at home with me. The time is getting shorter much too quickly for me!

Stage 1: Early Years

I like to apply this poem to three different stages of a woman's life. The first stage is the early years of marriage (vv. 13-17), then the mid-life years (vv. 18-22), and then the later years of marriage (vv. 23-27). I believe that considering this poem as stages will free you from false guilt.

The Problem of Comparison

When I think back to the first years of marriage, I was enthusiastic about every aspect of married life. I wanted to be the best cook, the best housekeeper, and the most godly woman in my husband's church. Unfortunately, I always seemed to find other women in the church who did more, knew more, and had it all together. No matter how hard I tried, when I compared myself with others, I fell short.

One woman in particular was very involved in our women's ministry and taught five different Bible studies. All of her children were grown and away from home, while I still had young children. Instead of seeing that she was in a different stage in her life, all I could see were my inadequacies. Fortunately, this godly woman kindly reminded me in very simple words that my time for more involvement would come.

In his poem, "My Angel Mother," Abraham Lincoln said: "All that I am, all that I hope to be, I owe my angel mother." Time and again, when successful men are asked who was most influential in their lives, they have stated that it was their mothers! Don't depreciate this significant period of your life when you may feel all you do is change dirty diapers or pick up toys.

Anytime we compare ourselves with others, we always lose. When we look at other people, we don't see their private struggles and personal problems that might cause us to be less envious. We should also ask ourselves about their stages of life. Was there a stage of life when they were not so involved? We may be comparing apples and oranges.

Comparing ourselves with others causes us to focus on what is lacking rather than on what God is providing right now. Focusing on God's priorities should be our measuring rods. Fortunately, I have been blessed with godly women mentors who have nurtured and helped me to grow.

> Anytime we compare ourselves with others, we always lose.

The Problem of Perfectionism

In addition to comparing ourselves with others, we may lose perspective by having unrealistic standards. Not only do we approach life with attitudes of perfectionism, but we also approach our marriages with the same attitude. We expect that our marriages will be blissful, our husbands perfect, and our children little angels. We may expect to be examples to others of perfect wives and mothers.

When my children were born, I wanted to be the best mother ever. I would talk to my friends and hear how they were raising their children and read everything I could get my hands on about parenting. I tried to follow all of this advice. My husband accused me of changing the way I mothered with every new book that I read—and he was right!

Perfectionism also affected my daily quiet time. I thought I couldn't have a quiet time if I didn't do it perfectly. My definition of a perfect quiet time was one hour with no interruptions. In a loving way my husband confronted me about this standard and encouraged me to spend time with the Lord, even if it were only a few minutes. I followed his advice, and now God has placed such a desire for Him in my life that I can't wait to be with Him, no matter how short or long a time it is!

Perfectionism can paralyze us so that we are overwhelmed by each day's demands. We hope to just survive the day rather than to look forward to what God is doing in our lives. God wants to use all the interruptions and chaos in our lives for His glory. His refining fire molds our character and develops us into the godly women that He so desires.

She manages her household.

In stage I, we are continually bombarded with so much information about our roles as wives and mothers that it is easy to get sidetracked. The Bible is still the best handbook we have on either subject. Whether you are a wife with no children, young children, or older children at home, God has a plan for this stage of your life.

Read Proverbs 31:13-17 and answer the following questions:
How could these verses refer to a younger woman?

_____

_____

What are some of her responsibilities? _____

_____

She selects wool and flax and works with eager hands.
She is like the merchant ships, bringing her food from afar.
She gets up while it is still dark; she provides food for her family and portions for her servant girls.
She considers a field and buys it; out of her earnings she plants a vineyard.
She sets about her work vigorously; her arms are strong for her tasks.
Proverbs 31:13-17

During the early years of marriage, the Proverbs 31 woman provided for everyone in her household. She made quality clothing for her family and selected their food with care. I am exhausted just reading this section! I have heard it said that rearing children and running a household are like holding a wet bar of soap—too firm a grasp and it shoots from your hand, too loose a grasp and it slides away. A gentle but firm grasp keeps it in your control.

 Do you neglect physical needs of your family? Check any that apply.
- ☐ mending
- ☐ cooking wholesome food
- ☐ occasional deep cleaning
- ☐ other? _____
- ☐ washing and folding laundry
- ☐ tidying the house
- ☐ cleaning out closets, and so forth

Living in Asia for over 16 years gave me a different perspective on verse 15. When I first learned that I would have daily household help as a missionary in the Philippines, it sounded too good to be true. After about a year, I found myself filled with resentment toward those who were helping me. I wasn't sure I wanted to provide for all their physical, emotional, and spiritual needs in addition to those same needs in my family. It was one additional pull on me that I wasn't sure I could handle. When I realized that God wanted to work through me to witness and minister to my household help, I was able to accept and develop this area of service to my Lord.

In addition to managing her home, the Proverbs 31 woman had a sharp eye for business opportunities (v. 16), and her investments yielded profits. However, her activities outside the home did not prevent her from caring for needs at home. Often women can get so busy that they sacrifice their homes. Not only can work pull us from the home, but our church work, Bible studies, shopping, and recreation can get in the way. Management of the home requires quantity of time as well as quality.

 Will you evaluate the way you manage your home? Does it bless your family and honor God? Place an X on the line below to indicate your management skills.

●————————————————————●

poor manager   adequate manager   good manager

81

In the early part of her life, the Proverbs 31 woman was clothed with strength (v. 17). She had developed physical strength along with strength of character. Don't forget to care for yourself physically during the demanding years of early marriage. Develop an exercise routine that may begin with walking, and progress to strength training and aerobic activities.

Include rest and sleep as often as possible. You cannot manage the home if you are exhausted. Periodic breaks away can help you maintain your sanity. When my children were young, often the only place I could get a break was in the bathtub! You will be surprised by how you gain perspective and receive God's encouragement during times of relaxation and refreshment.

As we close today, ask God to show you any inappropriate comparisons to others or perfectionistic thinking patterns that have weighed you down. Thank Him for the home you have to manage. Then, thank Him that He offers to lighten your burdens if you cast your cares on Him..

Cast all your anxiety on him because he cares for you.
1 Peter 5:7

Dear God, _____

_____

_____

Day 3
Stages of Life (continued)

She sees that her trading is profitable, and her lamp does not go out at night.
Proverbs 31:18

Today we are considering the mid- and later-life stages of a woman's life. If you are not yet in these stages, perhaps this study will help prepare and encourage you as you deal with the daily stressors of the early years. If you are in one of these stages, ask God to show you His best for these years as you seek to fulfill His purposes for your life as a couple and family.

The Mid-life Years of Marriage (vv. 18-22)

In the mid-life years, the Proverbs 31 woman continued to manage her household responsibly. Verse 18 tells us she evaluated her life and sensed that all was going well. Her work continued to yield profits, and she was considered financially secure. Verse 18 concludes with a statement that at first hearing might cause us to think the poor woman never got a good night's sleep. "Her lamp does not go out at night" speaks of availability, planning, and foresight. It does not mean that she did not sleep. It also referred to economic status. Not everyone could afford oil to light lamps. If you burned a lamp, you were a privileged member of society.

In Hebrew culture, a candle burning at night meant that weary travelers could stop and rest. Many times my home is not restful for the occupants—much less a weary traveler. What weary travelers need more than entertaining is a home where peace and tranquility reign and where they are valued as persons. Gourmet meals and beautiful decorations may say more about our need for attention and affirmation than about the needs of our guests.

List some ways you can make your home more peaceful. _____

_____

_____

I have had to work on being available just to talk—not judge or give advice—at night. By nature I am a morning person, and if I had my way, I would go to bed at 7:00 p.m. every night. I am convinced teenagers are night owls. They come alive when the moon is out and will share things of the heart only at this time.

Are you available to your teenagers or adult children? Being available means that you are available on their time schedule, not yours. Place an X on the scale.

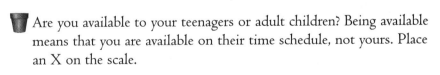

not available   usually available   mostly available

In verse 19 we find the Proverbs 31 woman spinning without using the wheel—a sign of diligence and thriftiness. She is not just buying for

You are a chosen people, a royal priesthood, a holy nation, a people belonging to God, that you may declare the praises of him who called you out of darkness into his wonderful light.
1 Peter 2:9

As God's chosen people, holy and dearly loved, clothe yourselves with compassion, kindness, humility, gentleness and patience.
Colossians 3:12

Warn those who are idle, encourage the timid, help the weak, be patient with everyone.
1 Thessalonians 5:14

In the name of the Lord Jesus Christ . . . keep away from every brother who is idle and does not live according to the teaching you received from us. . . . We hear that some among you are idle. They are not busy; they are busybodies.
2 Thessalonians 3:6,11

They get into the habit of being idle and going about from house to house. And not only do they become idlers, but also gossips and busybodies, saying things they ought not to.
1 Timothy 5:13

convenience but being very practical. We must not conclude that the Proverbs 31 woman encourages us to pursue wealth or to equate wealth with God's blessings. Rather, we are to pursue diligent work, make wise investments of our time and money, and use our resources wisely.

Verses 21-22 reference the clothing of her household. It's described as fine linen and purple. Purple is the color of royalty worn by one with dignity. She and her family were persons of noble character. Did you know that you are a member of a royal household?

 Read 1 Peter 2:9 at the top of the margin. Underline the royal household to whom you belong.

Read Colossians 3:12. Underline the items of clothing worn by a member of God's royal household.

The Later Years (23-27)

By this stage, the husband of the Proverbs 31 woman was seated among the elders at the city gate. His respected position was a tribute to his wife as well as himself (see v. 31). At this stage, she earned money from her merchandising business (v. 24). In verse 27 we are told that she continued to act as a responsible manager of the affairs of her household.

 Verse 27 states that idleness was not one of her characteristics. Summarize what the following verses say about idleness.

1 Thessalonians 5:14 _____

2 Thessalonians 3:6,11 _____

1 Timothy 5:13 _____

Being idle should not be confused with being rested. In each stage of life, God provides times of rest from physical demands; however, His rest does not encourage laziness or indulgence that keeps us from serving the Lord and others.

As she grew older, strength and dignity clothed her (v. 25). Her physical strength (see v. 17) was not diminished because of her hard work. Her strength of character had grown, as well. The result was wisdom that she shared with others (v. 26).

Read Proverbs 24:3. How does the Lord build wisdom in our lives?

_____

Read Proverbs 9:10. From whom do we get knowledge and

understanding? _____

Whether you teach a class or participate as a member of a study group, you share life lessons with others. You may instruct intentionally or unintentionally, but don't forget that people watch your example. It has been said that you may be the only Bible some will read. This stage is the time of life to concentrate on mentoring and encouraging younger women.

Read Titus 2:3-5. Underline the purpose for the behaviors Paul asked of the women.

Were you surprised that older women would have to teach younger women to love their husbands? Ladies, true love is something we develop through years of walking with the Spirit (Gal. 5:22). The word *love* in verse 3 means *fond, affectionate kindness, tender affection, companionable love.* It involves giving as well as receiving.

In Praise of Age
Some cultures revere and honor older women. However, in others older women lose their value in a society focused on youth and beauty. The charm and beauty of youth are temporary (Prov. 31:30). If you invest in looking younger, you are buying into the world's standard.

The Proverbs 31 woman received the praise of her children, husband, and works (vv. 28-31). The best compliment and her most important virtue was that she feared the Lord! Everything she accomplished can be attributed to her reverence for the Lord.

The Proverbs 31 woman smiled when she thought about the future. She didn't live under a cloud of fear; her life was committed to the Lord (see v. 30). Our fears and worries indicate whether we trust in God.

Have you benefited from considering the stages of life represented by the Proverbs 31 woman? Hopefully, you discovered many ways you resemble her. Probably you discovered some areas of weakness. God can use our recognition of weakness as a means of providing His strength.

By wisdom a house is built, and through understanding it is established.
Proverbs 24:3

"The fear of the Lord is the beginning of wisdom, and knowledge of the Holy One is understanding."
Proverbs 9:10

Teach the older women to be reverent in the way they live, not to be slanderers or addicted to much wine, but to teach what is good. Then they can train the younger women to love their husbands and children, to be self-controlled and pure, to be busy at home, to be kind, and to be subject to their husbands, so that no one will malign the word of God.
Titus 2:3-5

Circle ways you want to grow in modeling the virtuous woman. .

    trustworthiness   integrity   diligence

    wise financial decisions   physical strength   hospitality

    generosity   planning for the future   reverence for God

Now, ask God to develop you in these ways He has shown you.

> *Dear God,* _____
>
> _____
>
> _____

Day 4

Balance in Home and Work

She watches over the affairs of her household. Proverbs 31:27

Today we will look at two different roles of an excellent wife: home manager and marketer to the world. Each role easily has a life of its own and battles for our time and energy. We desire balance; at the same time, we are not sure where to find it.

    We must never forget that our primary relationship is with God. He is the one who gives us balance. Read Proverbs 31:10-31 again, and don't be tempted to skim these verses. Ask God to give you fresh eyes and new insights today.

Home Manager (13-15,19,21-22,27-28)

Recall from week 1 that you and your husband were designed to complement each other's gifts in establishing your home. The wife has the designated responsibility of managing the home.

Read Titus 2:5. Underline the word that describes the wife's work at home.

... to be self-controlled and pure, to be busy at home, to be kind, and to be subject to their husbands, so that no one will malign the word of God.
Titus 2:5

The Greek translation of "to be busy at home" is to watch over and be the keeper of the house. This rendering implies that the woman is to manage the home in a protective, watchful manner. She may consult with her husband, but she is not to manage him. However, she does have the ultimate responsibility to manage the home.

A godly woman is careful not to allow her outside activities to interfere as she manages the home. I have always struggled to find balance between my household responsibilities and outside involvement with the church, neighbors, friends, and community. With pulls in so many directions, we must remember that our primary responsibility after our relationship with God and with our husband is managing the home.

 Read I Timothy 5:13-14. What is the danger if we are not busy

managing our homes? _____

_____

They get into the habit of being idle and going about from house to house. And not only do they become idlers, but also gossips and busybodies, saying things they ought not to. So I counsel younger widows to marry, to have children, to manage their homes and to give the enemy no opportunity for slander.
1 Timothy 5:13-14

Paul cautioned women to avoid the dangers of idleness, gossip, and slander. You may not go from house to house spreading gossip, but do you allow it in your home through the media—radio, television, the Internet? Oh dear ladies, be careful what you watch and listen to as you go about your household responsibilities. Satan can use outside influences to negatively impact the way we manage our homes.

Does your home bring honor and glory to the Lord? God desires that our homes be a little taste of heaven on earth. Can you do anything to make the atmosphere in your home more godly? If so, ask God to give you the desire to honor Him by carefully monitoring the influences that come into your home.

As you manage your home, what is your attitude? Is your joy evident? Are you known as a grumbler? Now this is a tough one! No grumbling? Have you ever heard a mom say, or have you said, "All of you just think I am your maid!" Grumbling shows that we are not happy with what God has given us to do and and that we have an attitude of discontent.

Can you identify an area in which you can't find contentment? Will you give this area to the Lord? What positive action can you take to replace grumbling? Check all that apply.

☐ delegate responsibilities to other family members
☐ supervise family members' work without criticizing
☐ work as teams
☐ make household chores fun
☐ sing or memorize Scripture as you work
☐ pray as you work

Whether you eat or drink or whatever you do, do it all for the glory of God.
1 Corinthians 10:31

As home managers, we should work as if we are doing it for God. What a difference this focus can make in our homes. The evidence that a godly woman has managed her household well is that her children and her husband rise up and bless her (31:28).

Marketer in the World (16,18,24)

In an agricultural society, the Proverbs 31 woman was involved in earning the family income. From her crops, she made and sold linen garments and supplied belts to the tradesmen (v. 24). She was prepared for the next season and wisely invested what she earned. She was not isolated in the home but actively involved in the world around her.

This passage is not a command to work outside of the home or to earn money for the family. It does affirm her value both in the home and in the work place. She was a good business woman. The elders at the city gate praised her works (v. 31).

*She considers a field and buys it;
out of her earnings she plants a vineyard.*
Proverbs 31:16

Read the verses on page 89. Write the occupation of each woman.

Judges 4:4-5 _____

Acts 16:14 _____

Acts 18:1-3 _____

Working outside the home is one of many opportunities available to godly women, but it must not interfere with managing our households well. Some women have no financial need to work outside of the home. Others have to work to provide for the family. Some have special gifts or training that inspire them to serve others through their work.

Certainly, every woman should have the education and the training to provide for her family should the need arise. We must never presume that our husbands will always be our providers. Husbands die, leave their marriages with dependent children, become disabled, or lose their jobs.

Some wives may not have a choice about whether to work, but they can take heart: God will provide the strength for the tasks ahead. For the majority of her life, my godly mother-in-law raised three boys alone while working several jobs. She prayed continually for her children, trained them well, and through example and word led each one to a belief in God as the priority in his life. Her life was not easy, yet she placed her hope in God. Two of her sons are in full-time ministry with the third in an active lay ministry.

Other women have a choice about working outside the home, and it may not be clear to them what they should do. They may have bought into the cultural idea that work forms the basis of personal worth. Let me recommend that first you seek God's guidance and make Him the priority of your life. When God is your priority, He gives you His wisdom for each circumstance and decision you need to make.

Second, consider your husband's opinion. Some husbands want their wives to work at an income-producing job; others are quite opposed to the idea; still others struggle with the best decision. An attitude of willing submission places a high priority on the husband's counsel.

If you are in the work force, avoid the trap in which so many people find themselves. This trap encourages the employee to give the best to the company and use the leftovers for family and church. Do not get caught up in the rat race for success and recognition that has destroyed so many families. Let your income bless your family and not rob your family of your attention and loving care.

God has never limited women's opportunities, but the key is knowing what your God-given priorities should be. When our priorities are in line with what the Lord has for us, everything flows much smoother. We will be able to say no to things that don't fit His plans for us.

Number the following priorities in your life according to your honest evaluation, with I representing your highest priority.

_____ job outside the home	_____ husband
_____ God	_____ child(ren)
_____ church	_____ extended family

Deborah, a prophetess, the wife of Lappidoth, was leading Israel at that time. She held court under the Palm of Deborah between Ramah and Bethel in the hill country of Ephraim, and the Israelites came to her to have their disputes decided.
Judges 4:4-5

One of those listening was a woman named Lydia, a dealer in purple cloth from the city of Thyatira, who was a worshiper of God. The Lord opened her heart to respond to Paul's message.
Acts 16:14

Paul left Athens and went to Corinth. There he met a Jew named Aquilla, a native of Pontus, who had recently come from Italy with his wife Priscilla, because Claudius had ordered all the Jews to leave Rome. Paul went to see them, and because he was a tentmaker as they were, he stayed and worked with them.
Acts 18:1-3

Ask the Lord to show you if your priorities are out of order. Satan would love to bind you with guilt so that you feel discouraged or even hopeless. Remember that God will give you the strength and the ability needed for each task He requires of you. As you pray ask God to give you balance in your life.

Dear God, _____

_____

_____

In Joppa there was a disciple named Tabitha (which, when translated, is Dorcas), who was always doing good and helping the poor. About that time she became sick and died, and her body was washed and placed in an upstairs room. Lydda was near Joppa; so when the disciples heard that Peter was in Lydda, they sent two men to him and urged him, "please come at once!"

Peter went with them, and when he arrived he was taken upstairs to the room. All the widows stood around him, crying and showing him the robes and other clothing that Dorcas had made while she was still with them.

Acts 9:36-39

Day 5

Ministering to Others

She opens her arms to the poor and extends her hands to the needy.
Proverbs 31:20

God has given us much, and He desires for us to minister to others in order to give back a portion of what we have been given. Not only did the Proverbs 31 woman manage her home and earn income outside of the home, but she also had a ministry to those beyond her family.

Ministry springs from gratitude. (20,26)

The Proverbs 31 woman realized she had been richly blessed. As a result, she was involved in her community, caring for the needy in a compassionate and generous manner and faithfully instructing others.

Read Acts 9:36-39. Luke tells about a disciple named Dorcas who lived in Joppa. Write some of the things she did for others and the effect she had on their lives.

_____

_____

When she died, everyone began to tell Peter what this godly lady had done for them; "All the widows stood around him, crying and showing him the robes and other clothing that Dorcas had made while she was still with them" (Acts 9:39).

Often, we can be so busy learning about God that we forget to put into practice what God has taught us. God faithfully provides many opportunities to do things for someone else if we take the time to listen to His gentle nudging. Ministering in the church should be motivated by gratitude for what God has done for us. Ministry involves love and concern for people rather than accomplishing a task.

 Evaluate your service in God's kingdom. Place an X on the scale.

●————————————————————————————●

task, circumstance focused   people focused

Is there someone special on your heart to whom God would have you minister? If so, what do you think He would have you to do?

_____

My local church is like yours, I am sure—filled with many service opportunities. We have an outreach to a retirement home and bereavement ministries to those who have lost loved ones. Some deliver flowers to those who need a word of encouragement. Our church sponsors an active women's ministry that involves many women in teaching and leadership roles. We also send mission groups to foreign countries to tell others about Jesus and to show them His love and kindness.

Our homes are also avenues of service. A small home—if love is shown—is a great mansion to a needy soul. God brings people into our lives, purposely placing them within reach of our loving concern. Mercy is a gift of the Holy Spirit (Rom. 12:8). That does not mean that those of us who do not have this spiritual gift should not be serving. We are each to serve others. In the Bible women served alongside the men. They taught, prophesied, and ministered to those in need (see Mark 15:40-41; Acts 21:8-9; Rom. 16:1,6,12; Phil. 4:3).

The best prescription when you are feeling depressed—or just sad and unmotivated— is to do something for someone else. Often we are so

> The best prescription when you are feeling depressed—or just sad and unmotivated— is to do something for someone else.

focused on ourselves that we don't even know that there are others hurting just as much as we are or maybe even more.

A dear friend of mine who had just lost a baby related this story. She felt that a dark cloud had settled permanently over her life and family. To lose a child is probably one of the most difficult trials that one can face.

One day she was running errands and stopped her car at a traffic light where a large crowd was crossing the street. Suddenly it occurred to her that even though you could not see the hurt on their faces, just as you could not see the hurt on her face, probably many in that crowd were facing difficulties. She realized that many of these people did not know her Savior and therefore didn't have His great power and peace to cope. This insight made a difference in how she viewed ministry. From that time forward, she saw ministry opportunities on almost every corner. Eventually, God led her to a place of leadership where she could directly help women find encouragement from the Lord and the strength to just take the next step.

 Do your eyes see the needs of those around you? What are some ministries in your church and community in which you could volunteer? Is there someone you can ask for more information?

_____

_____

Ministry requires trust in God.

The Scriptures contain many examples of women who trusted God. In Exodus 15 Miriam led the nation of Israel in praise to God (vv. 20-21). In Judges 4 Deborah was a military advisor. Queen Esther was willing to sacrifice her life to save her people (Esth. 4).

Charm is deceptive, and
beauty is fleeting;
but a woman who fears
the Lord is to be praised.
Proverbs 31:30

 What quality produces a woman of excellent character? Read

Proverbs 31:30. List the quality._____

She is dedicated to God and has no fear of the future for her faith and hope are in the Lord. She displays her faith through her actions: she does all that the Lord her God commands. The fear of the Lord is a reverence and respect for God. When we realize who God is, we then come before Him with a humble spirit.

Matthew 6:33-34 gives us the prerequisite to living a life without anxiety. We are to seek God and His kingdom before all else! In other words, our relationship with God is our priority. When we love the Lord above all else, we are more concerned about pleasing Him than others. We seek to obey Him and spend time in fellowship with Him.

Do you desire to live a life of faith? First, ask God to increase your love for Him. Second, trust God to do His perfect will in your life. Third, commit your way to the Lord.

Read Proverbs 3:5-6. Let me challenge you to memorize it. Write the verse on a card that you can display on a surface such as a mirror or refrigerator that you see daily. Each time you look at the card tell God you trust Him with your current source of worry.

God will direct you every step of the way—even when you don't understand. He will carry you when you can no longer take another step.

Read Psalm 37:4-6 and summarize what these verses say to you personally.

_____

_____

You are in the process of becoming a woman of virtuous character. This week, you have probably noticed attitudes or behaviors you need to change. We change one step at a time. Ask God to show you one action you could take in the following week. Commit it to the Lord as you write your prayer.

Dear God, _____

_____

_____

Seek first his kingdom and his righteousness, and all these things will be given to you as well. Therefore do not worry about tomorrow, for tomorrow will worry about itself. Each day has enough trouble of its own.
Matthew 6:33-34

Trust in the Lord with all your heart and lean not on your own understanding; in all your ways acknowledge him, and he will make your paths straight.
Proverbs 3:5-6

Delight yourself in the Lord and he will give you the desires of your heart. Commit your way to the Lord; trust in him and he will do this: He will make your righteousness shine like the dawn, the justice of your cause like the noonday sun.
Psalm 37:4-6

Godly Communication

This week you will learn to

- communicate a clear message;
- be a more reflective listener;
- discipline your thought life;
- avoid hurtful words;
- cultivate healing words.

A recent survey of young unmarried adults indicated that the most important quality they were looking for in marriage was a soul mate. They desired someone with whom to share the future—both the good times and the tough times, the hurts and disappointments as well as the successes and joys. They wanted a mate who would encourage them and help make them a better person. At the heart of these desires was the ability to communicate at a deep level.

We all want to be heard, or more specifically, our hearts want to be heard. Problems occur when no one is willing to listen. Lack of effective communication is the number one reason couples seek counseling. Couples may be talking but not connecting, and certainly not connecting in a God-honoring way. Without a doubt, effective communication is one of the most vital ingredients in a successful marriage.

So what is effective communication? Good communication is the art of sending and receiving a clear message. No matter how long we have been married, we always have room for improved communication. The quantity of words does not necessarily improve communication. Often, our words lead to misinterpretations or defensiveness. They may wound the other person.

The solution is not to talk less! All of us continuously send and receive messages from others, even when we aren't verbally speaking. In fact, it is impossible not to communicate. Everything about us communicates in either positive or negative ways. We communicate even when we try not to because our silence communicates a message. What we need is quality communication. This week we will review communication principles that we can apply to our marriages and also to other situations and relationships.

Day 1

Clear Away the Fog

A man finds joy in giving an apt reply—and how good is a timely word!
Proverbs 15:23

I heard a story about an elderly couple who were celebrating their golden anniversary. Family came in from near and far, and they were enjoying a delicious meal. The husband, quite touched by this occasion, motioned to get everyone's attention. He began to give a glowing account of their years together and closed with these words to his wife. "After 50 years I've found you tried and true!"

Everyone smiled approval, but his hearing-impaired wife wasn't sure what he said and asked him to repeat it. "AFTER 50 YEARS I'VE FOUND YOU TRIED AND TRUE!" His wife looked shocked and hurt and then replied, "Well, let me tell you something—after 50 years I'm tired of you, too!"

Have you been there? I have! I sometimes try to communicate one very positive thing to my husband, and it is totally misunderstood. Communication is difficult, yet we desire communication at a deep and personal level. No doubt, communication is the lifeblood of a relationship.

Accept your reality.

Most of us enter marriage with the expectation that we will be able to share our life experiences with a significant other. Often our dreams don't match reality. As a result, we may fail to deal with the circumstances or trials we face because we refuse to give up our expectations.

What are we to do? We are to accept what is real and then acknowledge that God cares and watches over every detail of our lives. When difficulties arise, God is concerned with what is in our hearts, our attitudes, and our motives rather than with getting us quickly out of a situation. Here are some important ingredients of accepting reality:

1. Focus on the present.

We cannot focus on the present if we are focused on the past. Have you ever met someone who lives in the past? She will frequently comment, "If only I had done things differently ..." "If only I had married someone else ..." and, "If only I had known then what I know now ..."

When we give in to regrets about the past, we ignore the fact that God was working in the past just as He is working now. We must come to the point of acknowledging the sovereignty of God over every event in our lives—past, present, and future!

In thinking about the present, accept reality and then seek God's action plan. As long as we just wish for reality to change, we will not grow and mature our relationships.

 Will you give your past regrets to the Lord? Will you thank Him for His continual presence with you yesterday, today, and tomorrow? Write your prayer in the margin.

2. Recognize differences.

We come into marriage with two completely different styles of communication because our families were different. I was raised in a relatively quiet home where we did not raise our voices unless we were angry. To me, a raised voice was a sign of anger.

One day David and I visited an Italian family. When we walked in the door, everybody started yelling at each other. They were simply communicating their joy at seeing us and being with each other. But for me, the loud voices were upsetting. I had to learn that a raised voice did not always mean someone was angry.

 How did the communication patterns differ in your and your mate's family of origin? List at least one implication of these differences.

_____

_____

_____

We are also different in temperament. Some talk more than others; some are more analytical; others are more feeling-oriented. Men tend to be problem-solvers, while women often want to talk about their problems before reaching a solution. Recall from week 1 that God's good purposes in making us male and female are still valid today. Thank God for your differences. It has been said that if both of you agreed on everything, one of you would be unnecessary.

Clear Communication

Communication is the process of sharing yourself with another person so that the other person understands what you are saying. Communication is both verbal and non-verbal.

The classic model of communication involves two parts called encoding and decoding. Encoding is the process of putting the message in language and actions that make it an expression of our thoughts. Encoding is the sender's part. Decoding is the process that the listener uses to unravel and understand the message. Without getting bogged down in technical details, let's just point out that the nature of communication is such that it takes a team effort to accomplish—the combined efforts of the speaker and listener, writer and reader.

The one who says, "I just say whatever comes to my mind and that is just the way I am" is obviously a very self-centered and immature individual. That individual is asking to be misunderstood by others. Probably she listens to others with the same degree of self-centeredness and finds herself easily offended. She may be quick to blame others for their unkind words but oblivious to her own.

Begin your communication by considering the needs of the other person, not your own desires to get something off your chest. Communication is a two-way street. The mature individual does not insist that others understand her, but tries instead to better understand others. Included in the prayer of St. Francis of Asisi, are these words.

Oh, Divine Master, grant that I may not so much seek
... to be consoled as to console;
... to be understood as to understand;
... to be loved as to love.

Pick the right time to talk. If your husband is tired, has had a stressful day, or is ill—that is not the time to talk!

 Reread today's Scripture from Proverbs 15:23. Underline the adjectives Solomon used to describe finding the timely word.

One weekday Amy and I had gone shopping for school supplies. When we got home I started dinner, and then realized the store had given us

> **Communication**
> The process of sharing yourself with another person so that the other person understands what you are saying

A man finds joy in giving an apt reply— and how good is a timely word!
Proverbs 15:23

the wrong size of one of the items. Since Amy needed the item the next day, I knew I had to exchange it immediately. At that moment, David walked out of his home study, having just finished preparing a sermon.

Hurriedly, I explained my dilemma and told David what he needed to do to keep dinner from burning. About five minutes later, David turned to Matthew and asked, "What did Mom say?"

Matthew repeated my words. "Thanks, Matt," David said, "I didn't get a word of it."

"That's because she told you how she felt at the same time she told you what to do." Matthew's profound insight illustrates a key difference between men's and women's communication. When there is too much emotion in a message, a man may not "hear" the information. Women tend to have a greater capacity to express and sort through emotions.

To send a clear message, we need to consider the words we use, the way we say them, and our nonverbal communication. Experts tell us that only 7 percent of our communication is verbal but 35 percent comes from the tone of voice that we use, and the remaining 58 percent is sent through our body language. In other words, our eye contact, facial expressions, posture, and body movement all communicate non-verbal messages.

 What is a typical body language message you and your husband

send? _____

Foggy Communication

Often one or more of these parts of communication fog the message. For example, our words may indicate love and respect, but our voice tones and our body language show anger. When two different messages are sent, most of the time the negative message will be received and heard over the positive message.

When I am in the United States, one of my favorite activities is to go to a realtor's open house. I enjoy seeing the house plans and decorations. I also like to imagine my furniture in the house. One Sunday afternoon David and I were looking at a house in a new subdivision, and I said to him, "Wouldn't our piano look beautiful in this corner? I think this house plan would really suit our family and our lifestyle."

My husband quickly responded, "We can't afford it. You know this house is out of our price range." What happened in this situation? David heard what I said, but the message he received was that I was unhappy with him because we couldn't afford this house. That's not at all what I meant, but it was what David heard. A message can easily come through other people's filters differently than what was intended.

 Do you remember a time when your words were misunderstood by your husband? Could you have communicated more clearly? How?

_____

Be prepared to share ideas for clearer communication with your group at your next session.

Day 2
Change Your Focus

He who answers before listening—that is his folly and his shame.
Proverbs 18:13

A part of improving our communication is changing our focus. The focus in communication should not be on us—just expressing our hurts, hopes, and expectations. To truly communicate with your husband on a heart level, you need to develop an awareness of his needs. I am convinced that most wives have very little idea about the intense yearnings and hurts that their husbands hold inside. Your husband may give the impression that he's OK. "I can handle it all on my own." This apparent altogetherness is not always what is going on deep within.

 What difference would it make in your conversation if your focus were on your husband's needs? Write your answer in the margin.

Improve your listening skills.
Boy Scouts are taught to do a good deed every day. But have you heard of the Boy Scout who helped an old lady cross the street she didn't want to cross? He was so eager to do a good deed that he didn't consider her needs. Focusing on your husband's needs does not mean focusing on the

needs that you think he has or should have. It requires getting close to him and seeing life from his perspective. It requires listening to him speak about what worries him, what irritates him, what thrills him, what excites him, and so forth. It requires getting close enough to him to begin to understand what makes him tick.

When Amy was small, she loved to play with dolls. Many interesting conversations between the dolls came from her active imagination. As I listened to her play, I could tell that the boy dolls were drawn into a four-year-old female world. I never once heard those boy dolls say, "I think I'll just veg out and see what is on TV." Or, "I'm going fishing tomorrow morning." In her make-believe world, the men didn't hunt, fish, play golf, watch football, or go to hardware stores.

If we try to treat grown people like dolls, neatly fitting into our expectations of what they will do and say, we will be in for a rough time communicating with our mates. Let me say again, a self-centered perspective with an undisciplined mind connected to an undisciplined mouth will hurt a lot of feelings. That type person is also going to be easily offended by others.

 Have you ever treated your husband as though he were a doll fitting into your female world? (circle)   yes   no

List one way to affirm his masculinity and identity apart from you.

A self-centered person misses the blessing that comes from building up others. You can encourage your spouse if you affirm him as the person God created him to be—not as you might want him to be. When we act in unselfish concern for another person, we become a witness to the love of God. Love builds us up, and it is God's love that changes people.

Seeing your husband through God's eyes makes all the difference in the quality of your communication.

Seeing your husband—with all his unspoken fears, insecurities, heartaches, and joys—through God's eyes makes all the difference in the quality of your communication. I am so thankful that although God sees me with all my scars and insecurities, He still loves me.

How long has it been since you said your husband's name the way you said it when you were dating? His name was the sweetest name to your lips. Focus on him when you talk; be a good listener; ask open-ended questions that require a complete answer (How did you feel about that?)

rather than closed questions that can be answered in one word (How was your day? Fine.).

Recall the questions that you were to have asked your husband (see page 42). If you have not completed this exercise, sit down with your husband and begin the process of getting to know him better.

Much of our conversation falls on deaf ears, and much of what is said to us also falls on deaf ears. Listen to conversations between married couples; they are often dialogues of the deaf. We all like to talk, but few like to listen. One of the greatest gifts a wife can give her husband is the gift of listening—actively showing love and concern. If he feels heard, he receives the message, *I must be worth hearing.* If he is ignored, the message he receives is, *I must be boring,* or *She really doesn't care what I think.*

When your husband comes home from work, are you busy preparing dinner and helping the children with homework, while talking to a friend on your cell phone? Women are usually able do several things at once, but our husbands need us to listen to them exclusively. When we are doing several things, are we communicating that we really care about their day? Probably not. We cannot discuss good communication without discussing the importance of listening.

> Conversations between married couples are often dialogues of the deaf.

Practice reflective listening.

If you have really listened to your husband, you will be able to accurately repeat what he was saying to you along with what you think he may have been feeling. This process is called reflective listening. The focus is empathy—not just mechanically repeating the words that were spoken.

There is a difference between hearing and listening. Hearing is gaining content or information for your own purposes. You are usually more concerned about what is going on inside of you during the conversation. Reflective listening includes listening not only to your husband's words but to his body language. You are listening with your husband's needs in mind, not just your own. You are not thinking about what you are going to say next instead of what is presently being communicated.

When listening reflectively, accept what is said without attempting to judge or to test the motives. You may not agree with the content, but if you react to the content or tone of voice, you may miss the entire meaning. Remember: your goal is understanding, not agreeing.

*This is why I speak to them
in parables:*

*"Though seeing, they do
not see;
though hearing, they do
not hear or understand.
In them is fulfilled the
prophecy of Isaiah:
"'You will be ever
hearing but
never understanding;
you will be ever seeing
but never perceiving.
For this people's heart has
become calloused;
they hardly hear with
their ears,
and they have closed
their eyes.
Otherwise they might see
with their eyes,
hear with their ears,
understand with
their hearts
and turn, and I would
heal them.'"*

Matthew 13:13-15

Read Matthew 13:13-15. How did Jesus characterize the people of

His day? _____

When Jesus talked about the people's hearing, He pointed to their eyes as well as their ears. When our eyes and our ears are closed, we are unwilling to learn. We can conclude that if by our own choice we can decide not to listen, then by our choice we can ask the Lord to open our eyes, ears, and especially our hearts to truly listen to our husbands.

In these verses (see page 103), how does God listen to us?

Psalm 34:15-18 _____

_____

Psalm 116:1-2 _____

_____

Jeremiah 33:3 _____

_____

God listens with His eyes and ears. He listens with the purpose of helping us. He inclines towards us, which shows His concern—He doesn't want to miss a detail of what we are saying. Most importantly, God listens willingly because He loves us.

How can you become a better listener? First, learn how to listen with your whole body. Much communication goes on that is nonverbal. When we listen with the entire body, we communicate interest and concern.

Second, observe your husband. Learn when he is anxious and how his body expresses this emotion. Study your husband. Ask God to develop a deep desire within you to truly know and listen to him.

Third, learn how to repeat what your husband is saying and to express to him what feelings you hear. This practice doesn't come naturally and definitely requires patience. Are you willing to listen no matter how long it takes? Would you describe yourself as someone who eagerly awaits what your husband has to say? Solomon instructed us to listen patiently

(Prov. 18:13). He pictured someone who is more anxious to listen than to express personal opinions.

Will you practice listening skills with your husband this week? Record in the space below what you learned about your husband by just listening. Remember, use your eyes as well as your ears.

_____

_____

_____

_____

Ask God to give you spiritual eyes and ears to hear Him, as well.

Dear God, _____

_____

_____

Day 3
Train Your Mind

Let the words of my mouth, and the meditation of my heart, be acceptable in thy sight, O Lord, my strength, and my redeemer. Psalm 19:14, KJV

I memorized these words as a child, and they have never left me. I am so thankful for parents who emphasized Scripture memorization, for this particular verse is continually part of my inner conversations. As I attempt to work through my feelings about people and events, this verse keeps me in check. Otherwise, my unacceptable thoughts creep into my communication with my husband.

The eyes of the Lord are on
the righteous
and his ears are attentive
to their cry;
the face of the Lord is
against those who
do evil,
to cut off the memory of
them from the earth.
The righteous cry out, and
the Lord hears them;
he delivers them from
all their troubles.
The Lord is close to
the brokenhearted
and saves those who
are crushed in spirit.
Psalm 34:15-18

I love the Lord, for he heard
my voice;
he heard my cry
for mercy.
Because he turned his ear
to me,
I will call on him as
long as I live.
Psalm 116:1-2

"Call to me and I will
answer you and tell you
great and unsearchable things
you do not know."
Jeremiah 33:3

The Problem with Negative Thoughts

A wife who continually dwells on her husband's words—why he said it, second-guessing his motives—will most assuredly damage her marriage relationship. She may find it all too easy to read between the lines of what he says or does not say. "He says he loves me, but I think he just means ..." "He says he has done nothing wrong, and I can't prove it, but what about ..." "He's not been speaking to me lately; he must be feeling guilty about ..." "He's being nice to me; he must want something ..."

Have you ever dwelled on negative thoughts? I know I have. One very important biblical principle for dealing with an overactive mind is found in I Corinthians 13:5 and 7. Paul states that love "thinketh no evil" and "believeth all things."(KJV) When you constantly question what your husband means by his words or his motives, you violate this principle of love. When I fail to accept what a person says and does at face value, I am essentially saying that person is a liar. At this very moment, I need to stop my imaginative thinking and ask myself, *what is true?*

Does God know our thoughts and motives? Match the following Scriptures with the descriptions on the right.

____ Psalms 139:23-24   a. God exposes our motives.

____ Proverbs 24:12   b. God weighs the heart.

____ I Corinthians 4:5   c. God judges our thoughts.

____ Hebrews 4:12-13   d. Search me God; know my heart.

God knows our thoughts. Our part is to admit them to ourselves and to God. We can approach God with confidence that He will provide every resource we need to change negative thoughts.

Read Romans 8:5-7. Underline what those who live according to the sinful nature set their minds on. Circle what those who live by the Spirit set their minds on.

The mind controlled by the Spirit has life and peace. Notice that the sinful mind is hostile and unsubmissive to God.

Those who live according to the sinful nature have their minds set on what that nature desires; but those who live in accordance with the Spirit have their minds set on what the Spirit desires. The mind of sinful man is death, but the mind controlled by the Spirit is life and peace; the sinful mind is hostile to God. It does not submit to God's law, nor can it do so.
Romans 8:5-7

Discipline your thoughts.

What thoughts fill your mind? A healthy thought life that brings honor and glory to God comes from having a close relationship with God. This relationship causes us to want to honor Him in everything.

 Is it possible for us to discipline our thoughts? Yes it is. We are commanded to do so. Read 2 Corinthians 10:5. Which thoughts are we to make obedient to Christ?

Philippians 4:8 is to be the standard for our thought life. Every thought that is permitted to enter our minds should meet these qualifications. In addition to putting negative inner conversations out of our minds, we must replace them with the truth (pure, lovely, whatever is admirable, and whatever is excellent). We must remember that our inner conversations will determine our outward behavior and words.

First Peter 1:13 commands us to prepare our minds for action. This battle for self-control will take mental exertion. Our thoughts have to be actively and purposefully focused. We can't just ignore them; we have to be on the offense.

So, how do we learn to control our thoughts? The first step is to be aware of them. Keep a journal, and write down your most recurring thoughts. Label them as positive or negative, helpful or hurtful. This process may be time consuming, but it is very helpful.

Another way to eliminate automatic thoughts is to answer them by quoting Scripture that interrupts negative thinking patterns. I highly recommend memorizing any of the Scriptures you have studied today.

Keep the goal in mind.

 Read Philippians 2:2-8 in your Bible. Who is our model for godly

thoughts and motives? _____

We are to have the mind of Christ. Being like-minded refers to motives, goals, and aspirations. We are to please God in everything—including our thoughts. We are striving to emulate Christ Himself—His attributes and His character. This requires a single-minded focus.

We demolish arguments and every pretension that sets itself up against the knowledge of God, and we take captive every thought to make it obedient to Christ.
2 Corinthians 10:5

Finally, brothers, whatever is true, whatever is noble, whatever is right, whatever is pure, whatever is lovely, whatever is admirable— if anything is excellent or praiseworthy—think about such things.
Philippians 4:8

Therefore, prepare your minds for action; be self-controlled; set your hope fully on the grace to be given you when Jesus Christ is revealed.
1 Peter 1:13

Let me share some Scriptures that can encourage you in seeking to have the mind of Christ. Write these verses on cards that you can carry with you. Beside each verse, write an application for your life.

Psalm 19:14   Luke 1:37

Psalm 32:8   2 Corinthians 12:9

Isaiah 40:31   Philippians 1:6

When an undisciplined mind is connected to an undisciplined tongue, unwholesome speech surely results! Recall from 2 Corinthians 10:5 (p. 105) that as believers we have divinely given power to take thoughts captive. This verse assures us that God can give us power to overcome negative thought patterns that lead to speech that wounds others.

As you pray, give God control of your thought life. Ask Him to bring to mind thoughts that displease Him. Confess these. Thank Him for His constant presence and power. Tell Him you desire the mind of Christ.

> *Dear God,* _____
>
> _____
>
> _____

Day 4

Avoid Hurtful Words

The wise woman builds her house, but with her own hands the foolish one tears hers down. Proverbs 14:1

Many times I wish I could take back spoken words. When we speak hurtful words, it's difficult and sometimes impossible to repair the damage no matter how hard we try.

At home we may feel it is our right to say whatever we want. After all, if we can't say what we think at home, where can we say it? I have heard expressions such as: "Well, nothing will get done if I don't bring up the subject. If I don't take care of myself, nobody will."

Whether we like it or not, our words in the home set the atmosphere of the whole house. How would you describe your house? Is it a place where all who enter find peace and contentment? Or do they find unrest and chaos? As I ask myself these questions, I would have to honestly say that both would characterize my house at different times.

Types of Hurtful Words

1. Gossip

Have you ever met a notorious gossip? I have. Unfortunately, every church seems to have one. Prayer ministries have been destroyed by gossip, and people's reputations have also been destroyed. Not long ago, I met someone for the very first time, and by the end of the evening I knew, beyond a shadow of doubt, that she struggled in the area of gossip. She continually wanted to talk negatively about someone. When I would counter what she said with a compliment, she would think of something else negative to say. Her conversation broke my heart because the people she referenced were not believers. Her words had the potential to turn them away from God.

Don't repeat what you hear if you know it will bring harm to someone else. Proverbs 17:9 says, "He who covers over an offense promotes love, but whoever repeats the matter separates close friends." The same words could be said about our husbands. We gossip about our husbands when we share negative things about them with others or when we criticize them to our children. These words have the effect of separating us from them. We are not to use our mouths to hurt them. My rule is: if you can't say it in front of your husband, and if it doesn't build up his character, don't say it.

2. Lying

 Read Ephesians 4:25. We are to put off falsehood and to speak truthfully. Does truthful speech require us to answer in such a way that we injure the other person? Explain your answer.

Each of you must put off falsehood and speak truthfully to his neighbor, for we are all members of one body.
Ephesians 4:25

_____

_____

*The tongue that brings
    healing is a tree of life,
but a deceitful tongue
    crushes the spirit.*
Proverbs 15:4

Read Proverbs 15:4 in the margin. Underline the effect of deceitful words. Has someone ever crushed your spirit with deceitful words?

Tell how you felt. _____

_____

Proverbs 12:22 says, "The Lord detests lying lips, but he delights in men who are truthful." Honesty with our husbands begins with honesty with ourselves and with God. Ask God to show you your true motivation in communication. Is it to crush or wound? If not, speak the truth in love (Eph. 4:15).

3. Criticism

Just as some animals are poisonous, some tongues also spread poison (see James 3:8). Some poisons work slowly and secretly until they kill. Often we don't directly say hurtful words to our husbands, but we become masters at passive-aggressive words that slowly destroy. These types of words may appear on the surface to be benign, but they jab the heart of the person to whom you are speaking.

My husband and I established a nonverbal communication system: when one of us starts to say something that would be inappropriate or unkind, we place our hand on the other's knee. I have been so thankful for this gentle reminder.

Recently I counseled a woman who had seriously offended another woman. This person felt she was kind and gentle in her speech, yet her words were actually very hurtful. How can two good people totally miss each other in their communication? This can and often happens in our marriages. We seek to communicate helpful words, yet they are very hurtful, and we don't even realize it!

How can we express helpful and difficult words in a way that will bring healing and growth to our marriages? Our words should surround and cover our husbands with praise, admiration, and appreciation. When a wife's words are negative and insulting, it resembles not having a roof overhead (Prov. 21:9). There is no protection from the world's elements. Oh ladies, how our husbands need the protection of a wife whose words sooth and nurture.

It's not your job to change him; it is your job to totally yield yourself completely to a God who loves you and desires to meet all of your needs. Don't take this responsibility back from God. You can be assured, God will give you the strength to communicate loving words, even when you are not treated kindly. This is not easy, but with God's strength, it is not only possible, but you will be able to reply in a responsible manner. Our power source is the power of the Holy Spirit as we draw near in prayer for our husbands and for ourselves. If you are not well-treated, pray that God will change your husband's heart toward you.

4. Folly

Proverbs 12:23 says, "A prudent man keeps his knowledge to himself, but the heart of fools blurts out folly." We are not to speak words that are empty and thoughtless. Folly is the opposite of discretion. My prayer is that Proverbs 2:9-11 would be the goal of my communication.

The Source of Hurtful Words

Next week we are going to examine in greater detail the problems of anger, resentment, bitterness, and conflict. Today, however, I want us to concentrate on the heart issues involved in hurtful words. When our hearts are full of malice toward our husbands, our words will follow suit.

▆ Write the meaning of James 3:14 in your own words. _____

_____

Our mouths are connected to our hearts! You may ask, *What am I to do if my husband insults me? Can't I respond with a like insult? How can I be expected to be quiet?* Because we all face similar questions in difficult situations, the Bible gives us guidelines for this situation.

▆ Read 1 Peter 3:9-10. Why does Peter say we must keep our tongues

from evil? _____

_____

Peter was writing to Christians who were living in difficult situations. Persecution was rampant. Christians were losing their lives because of their faith. In addition, Gentiles had embraced the Christian faith, but their former lifestyles were as far away from the Lord as humanly

Then you will understand
what is right and just
and fair—every
good path.
For wisdom will enter
your heart,
and knowledge will be
pleasant to your soul.
Discretion will protect you,
and understanding will
guard you.
Proverbs 2:9-11

If you harbor bitter envy
and selfish ambition in your
hearts, do not boast about it
or deny the truth.
James 3:14

Do not repay evil with evil
or insult with insult, but
with blessing, because to this
you were called so that you
may inherit a blessing. For,
"Whoever would love life
and see good days
must keep his tongue
from evil
and his lips from
deceitful speech."
1 Peter 3:9-10

109

possible. Peter instructed them to live in harmony with others, showing compassion and humility. When they were insulted, they were to give a blessing. We are called to do the same. It takes much more strength and courage to bless someone when they have insulted you rather than to return an insult.

When we are careful about the words we speak, instead of hurting the other person, we will bring healing. Today's world really needs healing words. These words are the "tree of life." In other words, they bring life, "but a deceitful tongue crushes the spirit" (Prov. 15:4).

Will you examine your heart? Have you spoken hurtful words? What was in your heart when you spoke those words? Will you pray about your words? Will you give all of your rights and desires to the Lord? Will you ask the Lord to make you aware of your thoughts and the focus of your conversation? He will, for He is faithful and just. Write your prayer below.

Dear God, _____

_____

_____

Day 5
Cultivate Healing Words

The tongue that brings healing is a tree of life. Proverbs 15:4

I have defined *communication* as *the process of sharing yourself with another person in a way that brings about understanding.* Effective communication is accomplished only when the other person receives the message that you sent, both verbally and non-verbally. Communication can be effective, positive, and constructive; or it can be ineffective, negative, and destructive. While you may intend your message to be positive, it may be received as negative. So where do we begin to change ineffective communication?

Yesterday we reviewed types of hurtful words that have the potential to destroy relationships. As Christians we have an advantage over non-believers in that we can call upon the power of the Lord to control our tongues and to help us say what we should. Today we will look at helpful words that have the potential to strengthen relationships.

Healing Words

1. They build up.

What is the purpose of communication? Read Psalm 34:13-14 and Ephesians 4:29.

_____

Keep your tongue from evil and your lips from speaking lies.
Turn from evil and do good; seek peace and pursue it.
Psalm 34:13-14

Our purpose in communication is to do good, to build up the person to whom we are talking. We are to look for ways that we can verbally and non-verbally encourage him or her. We are not to let unwholesome talk come out of our mouths, which includes lies or exaggerations.

Proverbs 11:11 tells us that our words can tear down and destroy others, but when we bless others with good and gentle words, they are lifted up. Have you ever been discouraged and a kind word or look lifted your spirits?

Do not let any unwholesome talk come out of your mouths, but only what is helpful for building others up according to their needs, that it may benefit those who listen.
Ephesians 4:29

Describe a situation in which someone else's words gave you

encouragement. _____

_____

_____

Through the blessing of the upright a city is exalted, but by the mouth of the wicked it is destroyed.
Proverbs 11:11

Your husband probably works in an environment where he is continually being critiqued. Wouldn't you like to provide the type of home environment that builds his confidence—a place where he is valued and appreciated? It is sad when our homes are no more gentle than the workplace. When we tear down our husbands, we are tearing down ourselves also because we are to be one flesh. Our husbands need to know that someone loves them despite their weaknesses.

2. They are grounded in love.

The only way we become a person who encourages others is to let the love of Christ build us up. In the first chapters of Ephesians, the Holy Spirit, through Paul, emphasized being rooted and grounded in love—the love of God. As the church grows and as we grow as individuals, we do not lay aside love, rather love is an essential part of this process. The church "builds itself up in love" (Eph. 4:16).

We each have a deep inner need to be loved, but God, through Christ Jesus, more than meets this need. His eternal love expressed to us through the Word of God and the Holy Spirit's voice overwhelms us with the truth and reality of His eternal love. His love gives us peace, joy, patience, and every trait of the Spirit-led life (Gal. 5:22-23). His love frees us from continual self-centeredness, the opposite of God's love. Love is not self-seeking (1 Cor. 13:5).

Only through God's Spirit can we truly love another human being. After the fresh glow of infatuation wears thin, love for our husbands must come from God (1 John 4:7). If you are having difficulty speaking words of love to your husband, ask God for more love for him.

 Read 1 John 4:19-21. Substitute the word *husband* for *brother* as you read.

3. They offer wise counsel.

Our words are not only able to lift others up, but they can also give them added knowledge and wisdom (see Prov. 27:17). With our words we are to "sharpen" our husbands. That does not mean that we critique everything they do and say; it means that by nature of who we are and the words we utter, we help to shed light in whatever way is needed. When your husband feels he is valued and loved unconditionally, he will share more of what is in his heart. Home will be a safe place where your words truly seek his good and not your own personal gain.

4. They are thoughtful.

Healing words require thinking before speaking (Prov. 12:18-19; 15:28). We would save so much heartache if we would just follow this principle. "Reckless words pierce like a sword, but the tongue of the wise bring healing" (12:18). When I read this verse, my heart aches! O, how many words I have said to my husband and children that brought pain. What is the solution? Weigh your answers. When we answer rashly, others are

We love because he first loved us. If anyone says, "I love God," yet hates his brother, he is a liar. For anyone who does not love his brother, whom he has seen, cannot love God, whom he has not seen. And he has given us this command: Whoever loves God must also love his brother.

1 John 4:19-21

hurt because we have not thought through our reply, and we have not considered their feelings.

The difficult part is knowing when to speak. Often my words have been motivated out of a heart that truly wanted to help, yet that was not the end result. We all want our words to be helpful, but sometimes the best thing we can do is to be quiet (Prov. 17:27-28). This is definitely easier said than done. We must be careful what we communicate with our silence. Sometimes this message is what we want to communicate (I'm angry at you), and at other times we have communicated a message that was unintended (I don't agree with you). With our silence, we can communicate that we care for the other person and want to be available, or our silence can also communicate disinterest.

As a child, I remember that two of my Dad's favorite verses were Proverbs 17:27-28. He continually reminded me that silence was good and recommended that if I did not have anything beneficial for the other person to hear—just keep quiet. He reaffirmed continually that silence was a sign of confidence in the speaker's ability to communicate. I remember that he never felt like he had to give an opinion on everything. He was a great example of wisdom to me.

Another benefit of being silent is that it allows you to truly listen to the other person before speaking (Prov. 18:13). I had a friendship once that became very strained. I could not figure out if I had done or said something to offend her, so I asked. Her reply was that she found it very offensive that I never let her finish what she was saying. I then made a conscious effort to listen to myself to see if I was indeed finishing other people's sentences. I found that she was correct. Because my thoughts were always running ahead and solving problems, I never truly slowed down to listen.

A man of knowledge uses words with restraint, and a man of under-standing is even-tempered. Even a fool is thought wise if he keeps silent, and discerning if he holds his tongue.
Proverbs 17:27-28

5. They are kind and compassionate.
Kindness represents the counterpart of malice. Kindness is not prompted by the good that the other person has done, but by the good that God has done. It seeks to bring about the blessing of others even at our own expense. It does not seek to get even for the wrong done, but seeks to do good for God's sake.

Kindness is active! It is not just changing your thoughts or saying nice words. Sometimes you have to show kindness before your thoughts and words change. This is *agape* love in action. Kindness is a visible expression of God's love. Our husbands see God in us when we are kind to them.

Be kind to each other, be compassionate.
Ephesians 4:32, Phillips

Compassion is the ability to see the problem or the wrong deed from the other person's perspective rather than from our own. Compassion stems from kindness. Kindness seeks to bless our husbands, and compassion leads us to empathy for our husbands.

Our conversations can be full of grace if we understand that we are all imperfect (Col. 4:6). We also acknowledge that God has forgiven us of much more than we are ever required to forgive others.

A Tree of Life

Recall from Proverbs 15:4 that healing words are like a tree of life. Trees are important to the economy. They provide materials, prevent erosion, provide beauty, rest, and shade; and many bear fruit. Healing words are important to our marital economy!

If the roots of the tree don't go down deep, the tree will not grow in a healthy manner. If we are not rooted in the things of the Lord, then our words will decay rather than give life. To develop a strong root system we must meet with the Lord each day and learn from Him. We must permit the Spirit of God to fill our hearts with God's love and truth.

Do your words bring life and healing to your husband? What are some healing words that you can speak to him this week? Write your prayer, asking God to increase the quantity of your healing words.

Dear God, _____

_____

_____

Christ-Controlled Emotions

Most of us came expectantly into our marriages thinking that we were going to be able to share our soul's deepest longings—our hurts and our disappointments—with someone who would love and accept us no matter our faults and shortcomings. We hoped our husbands would be our confidants, our closest friends, and our lovers.

However, the depth of our intimacy with our husbands fluctuates. At times we feel very close to them, and then later we feel worlds apart. Such fluctuations are normal in healthy relationships. What should concern us is a marriage with more apartness than togetherness. Often, the sense of isolation or disconnectedness springs from damaged emotions.

Soon after marriage we received messages that wounded us—perhaps a cutting remark, a criticism, or even worse, our husbands' indifference. As a result, we may feel we can't trust them with our deepest feelings. So we erect barriers around our hearts that no one can break down. The barriers represent many layers stemming all the way back to childhood hurts.

Although the barriers are there, we still long for deep, interpersonal communication with the one we love. We also want our husbands to talk to us so we can truly know them on a deeper level, yet they are silent, absent, or both. The end result is two people living together but strangers on an intimate level. As a result, we may communicate negative words that solidify the barriers rather than tearing them down.

Oh ladies, God cares about your communication with your husband. He wants him to be your priority earthly relationship. This week we will discover that Christ wants to be Lord over our negative feelings so that we speak and act in loving ways. We will also look at what to do when we get hurt. Our focus will be on pleasing God for He is ultimately the One we most want to honor with our feelings, words, and actions.

This week you will learn

- the power of the tongue;
- appropriate ways to handle conflict;
- God's remedy for anger;
- the benefits of worry-free living;
- the blessings of a forgiving spirit.

Day 1

The Power of the Tongue

The tongue has the power of life and death, and those who love it will eat its fruit.
Proverbs 18:21

Have you ever wished you could put words back into your mouth? I certainly have! I have an especially painful memory of my tongue getting me into trouble while I was in middle school. My best friend for three years had done something to hurt me. To this day, I can't remember what it was, but I do remember what resulted. Another group of friends encouraged me to "tell her off." I followed their advice and publically scolded my friend in as dramatic language as I could muster. I'll never forget that look of pain etched on her face. I later apologized, but the damage was done, and we were never close friends again.

Unfortunately that was not the last time my words hurt someone else. A popular saying of children in almost every culture goes like this: "Sticks and stones may break my bones, but words can never hurt me." This saying is not at all true. In fact, I believe we can get over physical hurts much quicker than the hurts caused by words. In every counseling session I uncover a wound that happened a long time ago, caused by someone else's words. Usually someone very close to us uttered these words, and that is why they hurt so much.

Marriage is no exception. The words we communicate to our husbands have the power to either tear down or build up. These words are also used to influence others in what they think about our husbands. They can either be used in front of our children to build up their fathers, or they can be used to destroy their respect for them.

Today we will look at James 3:1-12. In chapter 1, James explained to his readers that the mature Christian is patient in trouble and trials. Then in chapter 2, he encouraged the mature Christian to practice the truth of God's Word in both words and deeds. In the third chapter, he expounded on the power of the tongue. He said what comes out of our mouths will show others if we have a true or worthless faith.

 Read James 3:1-12 now. In your Bible, underline or highlight the verses of particular meaning to you. Mark your place here. We'll come back later.

Apparently a lot of people who read James' letter wanted to be teachers. They were impressed by authority and great oratory. Teachers, though, must practice what they teach. In the home, if you are not practicing what you teach in front of your children, they will follow what you do and not what you say. Whether or not you are a teacher, verse 2 then says "we all stumble in many ways," and the sins of the tongue head the list. All of us will be judged by our words.

The Negative Power of Speech

The power of speech is one of the greatest powers God has given us. With the tongue, we can praise God, pray, teach the Word, and lead the lost to Christ. What a privilege! But with that same tongue, we can gossip, destroy people's reputations, and tell lies. James used vivid imagery to explain why controlling our tongues is the key to maturity.

How is the tongue like a horse's bit or a ship's rudder (Jas. 3:1-4)?

_____

_____

James identified two items that are small, yet they exercise great power, just like the tongue. A small bit enables a rider to control a great horse just as a small rudder enables the pilot to steer a large ship. The bit has to overcome the wild nature of the horse, and the rudder has to fight mighty waves. The bit and the rudder have the power to direct, which means they affect the lives of others.

The tongue is a small member of the body and yet it has the power to destroy and the power to do great things. Your tongue has the power to negatively or positively affect those in your household.

Underline the power of the tongue according to Proverbs 18:21.

List a positive way your tongue has impacted:

your husband. _____

other family members. _____

The tongue has the power of life and death, and those who love it will eat its fruit.
Proverbs 18:21

*I said, "I will watch
my ways
and keep my tongue
from sin;
I will put a muzzle on
my mouth
as long as the wicked are
in my presence."
But when I was silent
and still,
not even saying
anything good,
my anguish increased.
My heart grew hot
within me,
and as I meditated, the
fire burned;
then I spoke with
my tongue.*

Psalm 39:1-3

How did David describe trying to hold his tongue in Psalm 39:1-3?

☐ He tore it out.
☐ He muzzled it.
☐ He remained silent.

When David tried to hold his tongue on his own, he was unsuccessful. He tried so hard, but then when he spoke, the wrong words came out.

Reread James 3:5-6. How is the tongue like a fire?_____

_____

A fire can begin with just a small spark, and then a whole city is destroyed. I will never forget some of the fires that occurred in the Philippines. No one ever knew what caused the fires—probably a careless match or a cooking fire that was left unattended. Because the homes were made of either a grass-type plant or untreated wood, they caught fire quickly and were out of control within a matter of minutes. Homes were burned to the ground, and the families literally had nothing left and nowhere to go.

Words that we say to our husbands can be equally destructive. A small matter that could have been handled with little difficulty can be blown out of proportion, just by careless words. Fire can spread very quickly, and the more fuel you give it, the faster and farther it will spread. The more you criticize your husband, the easier it becomes. You reinforce a negative thinking pattern and feel your words are justified.

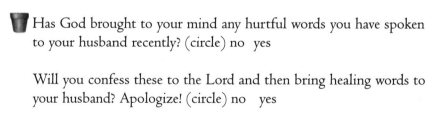

Has God brought to your mind any hurtful words you have spoken to your husband recently? (circle) no yes

Will you confess these to the Lord and then bring healing words to your husband? Apologize! (circle) no   yes

When? _____

God's Power at Work

If the heart is filled with hatred, Satan will light the fire. But if the heart is filled with love, God will smother negativity. It is your choice: to whom are you going to give the control of your words?

What image does Proverbs 18:4 use to describe wise words?

_____

The words of a man's mouth are deep waters, but the fountain of wisdom is a bubbling brook.
Proverbs 18:4

A fountain provides the cool and refreshing water that we need to stay alive. Water is life giving, and our words can give life. However, if water is not controlled, it brings much destruction and death to anyone who gets in its way.

 Reread James 3:11-12 in your Bible. What would happen to fresh water if a little salt water were allowed to flow with it?

_____

"Make a tree good and its fruit will be good, or make a tree bad and its fruit will be bad, for a tree is recognized by its fruit. You brood of vipers, how can you who are evil say anything good? For out of the overflow of the heart the mouth speaks. The good man brings good things out of the good stored up in him, and the evil man brings evil things out of the evil stored up in him."
Matthew 12:33-35

A few words, untimely spoken, can erase the many good words that have been spoken, just as a little salt water will make all of the water salty. Water also cleanses. Our words to our husbands can help to bring the living water of the Lord to them (see John 7:37-38).

We cannot expect to have control over our tongues and sweet words if we are not planting godly fruit. Read Matthew 12:33-35 in the margin. We must be rooted and grounded in the Lord. When words come out that hurt, we must examine our hearts. The question, *Who then can control the tongue?* becomes critical (see Jas. 3:8). When Jesus Christ controls our tongues, we do not need to fear that we will speak from a heart full of malice or selfishness.

 What did David pray for in Psalms 141:3-4?

_____

How do we keep our hearts from being drawn to evil?

_____

Set a guard over my mouth, O Lord; keep watch over the door of my lips. Let not my heart be drawn to what is evil, to take part in wicked deeds with men who are evildoers; let me not eat of their delicacies.
Psalm 141:3-4

Will you give God the right to control your tongue this week? As you get up every morning, pray, "God I give You my thoughts and my words today. Let them be pleasing to You."

Day 2

Handling Conflict

A quarrelsome wife is like a constant dripping. Proverbs 19:13

For many of us, conflict is connected with negative feelings, and so we try to avoid it. Because of misunderstandings about Christian teachings, many of us fail to see conflict as a normal and necessary part of a relationship. Do you believe that a sign of Christian maturity is agreeing with your husband at all times? If so, you probably have a negative view of conflict.

 What comes to mind when you hear the word *conflict?* (underline all that apply)

pain   fear   eagerness   dread   anticipation   resignation

Conflict started long ago in the garden with Adam and Eve, and it will continue until the end of time. If you hear someone say she has no conflict in her marriage, she is either stretching the truth or completely out of touch with reality. No two people are going to see everything alike.

Marriages are destroyed when we use unhealthy ways to respond to conflict. However, conflict can strengthen and mature our relationships. The key involves taking our conflicts to God and allowing Him to transform our minds. Your choice will determine to a great degree whether or not your love relationship with your husband will deepen and grow or whether it will be shallow and stagnant.

Choice 1: Ignoring

Initially, you may have chosen to handle conflict by just ignoring it. As more and more conflicts pile up, we just keep adding to the rubbish bins of our minds. Eventually, all those conflicts that have been put into the bin rot until the stench is so strong that we can no longer ignore their presence; and we explode, leaving a trail of destruction.

Choice 2: Avoiding

We may be aware of our conflicts and yet be unwilling to deal with them. We may postpone them by saying we would be glad to handle this problem later when we have more time to think. In today's fast-paced society, we can find many excuses to put off a conflict until it is too late and the hurt is so great that we consider separation as the only solution.

Many couples have one partner who responds by avoidance at all costs while the other attacks. If you are the avoider, you need to know the problem won't be solved by indefinitely postponing it.

Choice 3: Defensiveness

Are you married to someone who is defensive about every issue on which you disagree? Perhaps you are the defensive one. Defensiveness blocks necessary communication and builds up barriers to listening. Defensiveness fails to see the other person as a partner whose opinions God wants to use to broaden our perspectives and mature us.

Choice 4: Selfishness

The person who always has to have her own way has never learned that it is more blessed to give than to receive (Acts 20:35). Selfishness promotes a win-lose mentality that makes competition the primary method of conflict resolution. Win-lose is always lose-lose. Great marriages are never built on the foundation of selfishness.

Choice 5: Attacking

Some women think a good defense is a strong offense! They are quick to fight and usually start the battle. Often the attack includes words meant to sting and offend. Although they may win by such tactics, they promote discord and destroy unity.

 Write the word used to describe the wife in the following Scriptures:

Proverbs 19:13, Proverbs 21:9, Proverbs 27:15._____

Choice 6: God's Way

When we choose to see conflict through God's eyes as a great opportunity for increased intimacy, growth, and maturity, then we can approach conflict more objectively and open ourselves to truly communicating. When we see conflict through God's eyes, we are more likely to be motivated by love rather than fear. The process of growing in your relationship with your husband involves saying:

*A foolish son is his
father's ruin,
and a quarrelsome
wife is like a
constant dripping.*
Proverbs 19:13

*Better to live on a corner of
the roof
than share a house with
a quarrelsome wife.*
Proverbs 21:9

*A quarrelsome wife is like
a constant dripping on a
rainy day;
restraining her is like
restraining the wind
or grasping oil with
the hand.*
Proverbs 27:15

121

- I have issues that are important to me.
- I care enough about you and our relationship to risk confrontation.
  I care enough about you and our relationship to speak the truth in love.
- I don't lose when I'm proven wrong or don't get my way.
- I DO lose when I throw away an opportunity to learn, care, and grow.

Here are a few principles from God's Word about handling conflict.

I. Keep the temperature down! Proverbs 15:18

A hot-tempered man stirs up dissension, but a patient man calms a quarrel.
Proverbs 15:18

When we get angry easily, we will act in foolish ways and will increase the conflict rather than find solutions. Anger does not usually lead to understanding. When my children were young, I found that counting to myself before responding to an unacceptable behavior helped me maintain emotional control. I would tell my children that "Mommy needs a time-out." I had a special chair that I would sit in, and amazingly, the house would become very quiet during these times!

Eventually I replaced counting with Scriptures I had memorized. This method had unbelievable results! When God fills your mind with His Word, your heart rate slows down, and your emotions and words stay under control.

2. Think first! Proverbs 10:19

When words are many, sin is not absent, but he who holds his tongue is wise.
Proverbs 10:19

So many times I have looked back and wished I had taken a few moments to think before I spoke! That is all it would have taken—a few moments. When your focus is on meeting the needs of the one to whom you are speaking, then you will not be as quick to take offense. Conflicts can be avoided or remedied quicker by thinking first!

3. Make understanding your aim. Proverbs 18:2

A fool finds no pleasure in understanding but delights in airing his own opinions.
Proverbs 18:2

God will show you wonderful things that you normally would not have known just by the simple act of listening. You must enter into the conflict to understand and not to win. Don't just assume that you know how the other person feels. Ask them, listen closely, observe the eyes and other body language, and open your heart. Good conflict has no losers. You both win because you have come through this difficulty together and have deepened your understanding of how the other thinks.

4. Be a peacemaker, not a pacifist. Romans 12:18

A pacifist wants peace at any price. A peacemaker is willing to work for an equitable solution. Finding the best solution may take time and effort. It generally requires more than one attempt.

If it is possible, as far as it depends on you, live at peace with everyone.
Romans 12:18

In the following Scriptures, identify the peaceful way to handle conflict by drawing a line from the Scripture on the left to its teaching on the right:

Psalm 34:13-14   get rid of bitterness, anger, brawling, slander, and malice

Proverbs 12:18   be willing to overlook an offense; exercise patience

Proverbs 17:9; 19:11   be sympathetic, compassionate, and humble

Ephesians 4:31   turn from evil and do good; pursue peace

I Peter 3:8   avoid reckless words; use healing words

We are to be diligent in seeking peace. We are not passive, just hoping we will find resolution and reconciliation; we go after it; we pursue it. We are able to overlook offenses because we know that God meets our needs, and He is the One we are serving. All that we do is motivated by *agape* love. We strive to reflect Christ's character. We are anxious and willing to forgive, and we pick our words wisely.

5. Speak the truth in love. Ephesians 4:15

According to Proverbs 4:24, what are we to put away?

_____

Explain in your words what it means to speak the truth in love.

_____

Speaking the truth in love, we will in all things grow up into him who is the Head, that is, Christ.
Ephesians 4:15

Put away perversity from your mouth; keep corrupt talk far from your lips.
Proverbs 4:24

Don't block God's work in your life. To be a truly wise wife, let Him work in you and through you. Your gentle words bring life and health (Prov. 15:4). Trust in God and allow Him to direct you in His ways (Prov. 3:5-6).

Where are you today? Are you in the middle of a conflict? What would God have you to do about it? Do you need to apologize for a hastily spoken word? Do you need to use God's manual to help you in resolving a conflict? Seek reconciliation and peace. Spend a few moments today praying for God's perspective on whatever you are facing.

Dear God, _____

_____

_____

Day 3

Managing Anger

Let there be no more bitter resentment or anger, no more shouting or slander, and let there be no bad feeling of any kind among you. Ephesians 4:31, Phillips

Dawn had been an exceptional beauty when she was young. She had been born into a family of privilege and wealth, but for whatever reason (I could never ascertain why), Dawn never felt loved or accepted by her father. Eventually she married a wealthy man and produced beautiful children. They appeared to be the perfect family. Quite by accident, Dawn found out her husband had been having continuous affairs from the time of their engagement until the present.

In a fit of anger, she kicked out her husband and eventually divorced him. When I met Dawn, she was one of the angriest people I had ever known. She spent our time together recounting the wrongs of her father and husband. In her mind, they were totally responsible for her unhappiness. How my heart ached for her. I know I cannot even begin to imagine what it was like to go through the difficulties that she endured. However, my question for you today is this: who was responsible for Dawn's anger? Was it her father or husband? Today we want to look at the source of our anger and then what we are to do about it.

The Source of Anger

Anger has been described as a feeling of extreme displeasure, hostility, indignation, or exasperation toward someone or something. Synonyms are *rage, fury, wrath, resentment,* and *indignation*. Not everyone has experienced the level of Dawn's anger, but the feeling is universal. In every country I have visited, anger and the emotions stemming from it hurt others and wreck lives. Surely, none of us wants to become like Dawn, who was avoided by family and friends.

Are you aware that your thoughts influence your emotions and can fuel anger? Are you aware that your inner conversations affect your behavior toward your husband much more than your husband's actions? Are you also aware that what you say and how you say it is a direct expression of your inner conversations? Most people are convinced that outside circumstances cause their anger. Actually, our thoughts are the source of the anger.

> Your thoughts influence your emotions and can fuel anger.

I remember a woman who spoke evil against me and spread lies about my children. I found out later she acted out of jealousy. I knew as a Christian I was to love her and allow God to fight my battles. The Psalms of David became my personal daily prayers. I was able to control any outward sign of anger toward her, but inwardly, just seeing her caused my body (heart, stomach, muscles, thoughts) to agitate. I was convinced that I was helpless to control these feelings.

Was anger a normal and justifiable response to the way I was treated? Most of us would respond that our anger is caused by others. We must realize that others do not make us angry; their behavior reveals our inner anger that has built up over a lifetime! It is my observation that almost everyone resists admitting that they have a problem with anger; rather, it is someone else's fault!

Who makes you angry? Is it your husband? Your children? Coworkers? It is none of these. The one who makes you angry is yourself—your feelings, your thoughts, and your own imaginations. Let me illustrate. On the interstate highway, if someone pulls in front of me to exit, I may or may not blow my car horn in exasperation. Some days bad driving makes me angry; other days I dismiss it and react with calm and patience. I've even been known to pray for the bad driver. Same experience—different reaction. My moods, expectations, time schedule, and degree of restedness all play a role in my emotional control.

 At what times of the day are you more likely to be irritable? Does your irritability affect how you deal with the actions of others?

_____

_____

Dealing with Anger

The problem we face is how to deal with anger rather than letting it mushroom. You may be thinking, *How do I control my thoughts? I can't get out of my mind the hurtful things that were said or what he did to me. I'm not sure I want to forget; it may happen again! Why is it always me who has to change?* We all know that to bottle up or swallow the anger is not the solution; it will come out some way.

"In your anger do not sin": Do not let the sun go down while you are still angry.
Ephesians 4:26

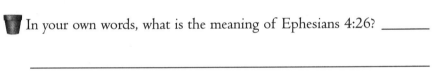 In your own words, what is the meaning of Ephesians 4:26? _____

_____

_____

Many will say that their anger could not be sin. Although we may not be able to discern righteous anger from sinful anger in every situation, the Scripture is clear that there is a difference. The "anger of man" which "does not achieve the righteousness of God" (Jas. 1:20, NASB) is based on our own self-centeredness. The anger which is an expression of God's righteousness is not self-focused. Jesus displayed this kind of anger when He cleansed the temple (John 2:12-25). Righteous anger is a reflection of God's moral standards. Godly anger is always under His control.

The sun is not to go down on our anger. In other words, it is not good to let unresolved conflict continue indefinitely. Each day is difficult enough without adding conflicts from the day before. Resolving conflict is worth your time and losing a little sleep. Practicing this principle involves more than settling a quarrel before going to bed. It requires settling disputes instead of letting them drag on and on, thereby not allowing anger and bitterness to set in. Otherwise, we give the devil a foothold into our thoughts and actions (Eph. 4:27).

Have you ever had a difficult person in your life who seems to bring out the worst in you? One day I was going to visit such a person, and I had asked the Lord to guard my tongue and let my communication be pleasing and healing. Initially, I was able to return good words for insults, and then I responded in kind. You see, the hurt was building up in my mind, and my focus changed from God's ability to guard my tongue to my own hurt. My thoughts became self-absorbed instead of God-focused.

According to I John 1:9, what are we to do with unrighteous anger?

_____

_____

If we confess our sins, he is faithful and just and will forgive us our sins and purify us from all unrighteousness.
1 John 1:9

We are to recognize our unrighteous anger as sin. Then we are to go to God and get His forgiveness and peace. Only God can replace anger with the fruit of the Spirit and give us the power to deal with difficult people.

Read Ephesians 4:25-32 again in its entirety. What grieves the Holy

Spirit? _____

_____

When we respond in anger and say hurtful or "unwholesome" words, this response grieves the Holy Spirit. The Holy Spirit is disappointed with us, just as a father is disappointed in a naughty child. Because we love God's Spirit, we do not want to disappoint Him.

What are we to get rid of according to verse 31? _____

_____

_____

What are we to replace these with according to verse 32? _____

_____

_____

This text gives us the good news that we don't have to be angry! We don't have to harbor resentment and bitterness. We can be free from the crippling effect that these attitudes have on our emotions, spiritual walk with the Lord, and on our bodies. This passage is all about change, and change is possible because of God's grace to us.

 According to this passage, when your husband has wronged you, what do you think Paul is asking you to do?

_____

We can cry out all of our grievances to God. He can handle it! Then we need to allow Him to show His power in our lives as we talk to our husbands. It is essential to talk to God first, or we may communicate hurtful words and actions that are coming from an angry heart. We must not allow our anger to turn into sin.

Putting off malice and bitterness and putting on kindness and forgiveness is the first step in the process of reconciliation. It is the prerequisite to reconciliation. Bitterness and malice are inward attitudes, sins of the heart. These produce wrath, anger, clamor, and slander. Clamor and slander are predominantly sins of the tongue. The cure for bitterness, anger, malice, and all of its fruits is forgiveness. Ephesians 4:32 takes care of all that Paul condemns in verse 31. We will discuss forgiveness in day 5.

Do you need to get rid of any feelings of anger, malice, or bitterness? Be honest. Allow God to begin the healing process.

Day 4

Living a Worry-Free Life

Do not be anxious about anything, but in everything, by prayer and petition, with thanksgiving, present your requests to God. Philippians 4:8

Recently I have had to go through what all mothers eventually go through, and that is having your first child leave home. Initially, I started thinking about all the things that could happen while Jonathan was away at college in the United States—all of the temptations, new experiences, and new friends. You see, for most of our life as a family, we have lived overseas. Experiences such as driving on the interstate or in busy cities were not part of Jonathan's growing up experience. Yes, he had many other wonderful experiences that were great preparation for college life, but driving was not one of them!

He chose a college that was a two-day drive away from any of our family, and his parents lived on the other side of the world. So, I had a choice. If I were going to live out Philippians 4:8, my thoughts needed to change. Jonathan had been prepared in many ways for college, and most importantly, he was prepared in the development of his character and integrity. He could make good decisions, and I knew that God was working in his part of the world as well as mine! To worry would be like saying to God, "I don't think you can take care of my son as well as I."

If my choice had been to worry about Jonathan, it would have affected my whole life in negative ways. I would have been distracted from my responsibilities and unfaithful in my witness to others. When we aren't functioning according to God's truth, we are hampered just as though we had a physical illness. You know you are limited when you're not healthy, even though you may still fulfill your responsibilities. Focusing on what is unhealthy can have a crippling effect.

Worry is an outgrowth of fear. Some life issues should cause fear: poisonous snakes, someone pointing a gun at us, falling from a great height. God placed fear in us as a survival response. However, the fears I named are legitimate and situational. Irrational fears, such as getting a deadly disease by touching a doorknob, are considered neuroses and are not part of a healthy person's mental state. To worry about something that hasn't happened as if the worry would prevent it is a waste of precious mental energy. These thoughts do not honor God, who is our refuge, our rock, our defender, and our protector (see Ps. 27:1).

> To worry about something that hasn't happened as if the worry would prevent it is a waste of precious mental energy.

Fears in Marriage

Many women live with the fear of their husbands' having an affair, of divorce, or of widowhood. Certainly, any of these fears are possible occurrences, since all of us are sinful and mortal. The fact that something can happen does not mean that it will happen. When we focus on our fears, we are telling ourselves that an outside possibility is a reality. We have allowed a maybe to dominate our present. The result is that we have robbed ourselves of the joy of today. What can we do to overcome these or other fears?

Once again we must look at Philippians 4:8 and consider that fear is rooted in thoughts about things that are not true. Trying to guess about what will happen and worrying about what might happen can too easily fill our minds with fear and keep us from focusing on our love relationship with God.

God did not give us a spirit of timidity, but a spirit of power, of love and of self-discipline.
2 Timothy 1:7

 Read 2 Timothy 1:7. What is the source of timidity, or fear?

_____

Underline the portion of this verse that tells us what comes from God.

Since God is not the source of fear, we are playing into the devil's hands when we give way to fear. Instead of fear, God has given us three very good gifts:

1. power—God is all-powerful. He has the power to care for us. Nothing is greater than God's power at work in any situation (see Ps. 20:7).
2. love—Nothing can separate us from God's love (Rom. 8:35). Since God is all-loving, nothing can happen to us that He does not allow. God will never act except in our best interests.
3. self-discipline—God expects us to discipline our thought life. We are not to be victimized by fear. It is within possibility that we can live a worry-free life (Phil. 4:6).

Fears lead to worry.

Therefore do not worry about tomorrow, for tomorrow will worry about itself. Each day has enough trouble of its own.
Matthew 6:34

 Underline what Matthew 6:34 says about worry. Why is this statement true, in your opinion?

_____

In no way was Jesus suggesting that we should not make appropriate plans for the future. Many of his listeners were farmers, and they knew they had to plant seed in order to reap a harvest months later. He was specifically addressing worry and fretting over things we cannot do anything about today.

For example, someone might worry, "Will my husband love me when I'm old and wrinkled?" If she lets that worry consume her, she will likely look old before her time! She could, on the other hand, focus upon ways she could love her husband today and let the future take care of itself.

It takes a very courageous person to let the future worry about itself, but through Christ we can be that type of person. Focus upon the good in life! Focus upon the present! Let God's love for you give you the confidence you need to live each day victoriously!

Read the parable of Jesus in Luke 12:16-20 in your Bible. What was Jesus trying to teach us in this parable? Compare His words with James 4:13-16.

_____

_____

_____

Listen, you who say, "Today or tomorrow we will go to this or that city, spend a year there, carry on business and make money." Why, you do not even know what will happen tomorrow. What is your life? You are a mist that appears for a little while and then vanishes. Instead, you ought to say, "if it is the Lord's will, we will live and do this or that." As it is, you boast and brag. All such boasting is evil.
James 4:13-16

Live worry-free.

When our daughter was about four years old, we thought we were going to lose her. In fact, so did the doctors. We know now that God has a special plan for Amy's life because this was not the first time that she was spared from serious illness.

When Amy was born, she had a mal-absorption syndrome. Even though we fed her well and took care of all her needs, she looked like a malnourished child. We were sent to a children's medical center for tests. We got a diagnosis, but it was given without any prognosis. When we left the clinic, we had no idea what Amy's future might hold. What the doctor and her parents didn't know at the time was that God had just healed her. We left the center not knowing what we were going to do, but she had no more problems from that moment on.

Then, when she was four, she developed meningitis and encephalitis. She was hospitalized and not given a good prognosis. As I sat by her bed, silently watching her when she was sleeping, or when I had to hold her down because of extreme agitation when she was awake, the Lord and I talked. I wanted her to be healed, and I pleaded with the Lord. I really can't describe what happened next, but in my heart, as I was seeking strength and guidance from the Lord, a peace came over me. I didn't know what would happen to Amy. I knew, though, that God cared more about her than I did. I gave her completely to His hands and His care. I realized that He may desire to bring her to Himself and I just prayed for the strength to handle whatever would come—whether healing or death.

Amy was taken to surgery to relieve the pressure on her brain, and again her father and I prayed for God's will and not our own. This was probably the most difficult prayers we had ever prayed! Amy did get better and even to this day there are no after-effects of her illness.

What happened in my life that changed my desperation to peace? It was seeking God's kingdom above all else. I was telling the Lord that I wanted His will in Amy's life before my will. In fact, what I had previously wanted was no longer important. Was I able to do this because I had a strong faith? Definitely not, for my faith was very weak at that point. It was because God was sufficient, and He was the only one in whom I could put my hope and trust.

Living a worry-free life requires that we give up our wills to the will of our loving Heavenly Father. It demands that we trust Him with everything—our families, our reputations, our lifestyles. It accepts the fact that He is Lord, and He has the right to give or to take back, to heal or to bring us home to Himself. A worry-free life is childlike faith in action.

Do you remember when your children were young and did not understand why you kept them from an open fireplace, or told them not to touch a hot stove, or allowed the doctor to give them painful immunizations? You acted out of love, but they interpreted your actions as unloving. In the same way, we can get so caught up in our selfish wants and desires that we rail at God when He seems to be saying no to our requests. Keep in mind that God always acts out of love. We must obey Him even when we do not understand His actions. One of His commands is "do not worry"(Matt. 6:25).

Do not be anxious about anything, but in everything, by prayer and petition, with thanksgiving, present your requests to God.
Philippians 4:6

List a worry you have not been able to give completely to God.

_____

Decide today that you are going to live a worry-free life. Turn your worries over to God. Claim the truth of Philippians 4:6.

DAY 5
Practicing Forgiveness

Be kind and compassionate to one another, forgiving each other, just as in Christ God forgave you. Ephesians 4:32

When I got married, I found it very difficult to apologize to David for inconsiderate words even though I loved him with all of my heart. David, however, would come to me and apologize for any wrong words or actions and without asking or expecting an apology from me. Every time he modeled asking for forgiveness, a pang of guilt would hit me. It took a long time, but I came to realize that I needed to approach David with the same humility.

Many of our problems could be averted if we would quickly and willingly confess our wrongs to each other. Hanging on to bitterness and vengeance resembles having a videotape planted in your mind that can't be turned off. Have you ever gotten a song in your head that you can't stop singing to yourself? We can do the same thing with the hurts that we hold on to and that eventually color our perspective of life. Forgiving turns off the song of bitterness and anger. Forgiving is the only way to stop the cycle of being in bondage to anger and bitterness.

False Beliefs about Forgiveness

We have many false beliefs when it comes to forgiveness. One of these is that time heals all wounds. Have you ever held on to a bitterness that is still with you 20 years after the event? 30 years after the event? Time may lessen the pain, but it does not heal hurts!

Another false belief is that forgiveness equals denying your hurt or pretending that your pain is minor. You may try to convince yourself that what your husband said is insignificant, but you are actually working against the forgiveness process. When you deny hurt, you deny reality.

A third false belief is that if you tell your husband you have forgiven him, then you have truly forgiven him. There is a difference between telling others that you have forgiven them and actually forgiving them. Forgiving your husband should begin in your thoughts and prayers and be a settled issue before you tell him.

A fourth false belief is that forgiveness always means you must continue to relate to the offender. If you have been abused, forgiveness

"Do not judge, or you too will be judged. For in the same way you judge others, you will be judged, and with the measure you use, it will be measured to you.

"Why do you look at the speck of sawdust in your brother's eye and pay no attention to the plank in your own eye? How can you say to your brother, 'Let me take the speck out of your eye,' when all the time there is a plank in your own eye? You hypocrite, first take the plank out of your own eye, and then you will see clearly to remove the speck from your brother's eye."

Matthew 7:1-5

will set you free, but you should not continue such a relationship. If you are in an abusive situation, refer to my counsel on pages 49-50.

🪣 Have you operated out of these false beliefs? (check one or more)
- ☐ Time heals all wounds.
- ☐ The hurt was insignificant.
- ☐ Saying the words equals forgiveness.
- ☐ If I forgive, I must stay in the relationship.

God's Standard for Forgiveness

1. God commands us to forgive. Matthew 6:14-15

Forgiveness is an act of the will. Are we going to obey God or hold on to our anger and bitterness? For many, anger and bitterness become a way of life they are reluctant to give up. Unforgiveness holds them captive just as though they were imprisoned.

🪣 Read Matthew 18:21-22. Underline how many times you are to forgive someone.

Read Matthew 18:35. Where does forgiveness begin? _____

2. God's forgiveness motivates us to forgive.

Because we have been forgiven, we desire to forgive others in obedience to God. God stands ready to forgive (1 John 1:9). Once we understand the depth of our sin and the distance it puts between us and God, and once we get a glimpse of the sacrifice of Christ on the cross, we should not hesitate to forgive others.

If we understand what God did for us and then refuse to forgive those who have wronged us, we are like the wicked and ungrateful servant Jesus described in Matthew 18:23-35.

3. Our forgiveness should be total and complete.

If Christ's death on the cross motivates us to forgive, it also empowers us to forgive. God's forgiveness in Christ sets the standard for our forgiveness. It should be total and complete just as Christ's death on the cross completely saves us from our sins when we believe on Him as Lord.

God did not selectively forgive us of some sins and not others. Some women have a hierarchy of sins: they will forgive some but not all. When

"If you forgive men when they sin against you, your heavenly Father will also forgive you. But if you do not forgive men their sins, your Father will not forgive your sins."
Matthew 6:14-15

Peter came to Jesus and asked, "Lord, how many times shall I forgive my brother when he sins against me? Up to seven times?"

Jesus answered, "I tell you, not seven times, but seventy-seven times"
Matthew 18:21-22

"Forgive your brother from the heart."
Matthew 18:35

you think about the cross and some of your own specific mistakes, aren't you glad that God doesn't pick and choose which sins He will forgive?

Often in counseling sessions, wives go down the list of all their husbands have done wrong. First Corinthians 13:5 tells us to keep no record of wrongs. When you continually dwell on the wrongs of your husband, in all probability you have not truly forgiven him from your heart.

[Love] is not rude, it is not self-seeking, it is not easily angered, it keeps no record of wrongs.
1 Corinthians 13:5

4. Forgiveness does not depend on the other person.

 Read Romans 5:8. Underline our condition when Christ died for us.

When God saw how lost and sinful we were, He initiated the contact, even though we were the ones who were in the wrong. Do you find it difficult to be the first to seek reconciliation, especially when you were the one who was hurt? To avoid intimacy or communication will just widen the gap and increase the hurt. Like God, reach out to the offender.

God demonstrates his own love for us in this: While we were still sinners, Christ died for us.
Romans 5:8

 What do you learn about forgiveness from Luke 23:34?

_____

_____

Jesus said, "Father, forgive them, for they do not know what they are doing." And they divided up his clothes by casting lots.
Luke 23:34

Although His accusers were unaware of their need for forgiveness, Jesus forgave. Many women comment, "I would forgive him if I knew he was truly sorry, but..." Release your husband from the debt you believe he owes you for the offense. Bundle your negative feelings; give them to God. You may say, *But he may repeat the behavior.* So do we! How many times do we confess a sin that we have repeatedly confessed to God?

 Recall Jesus' words in the Model Prayer (Matt. 6:12). What condition did Jesus put on our forgiveness by God?

_____

_____

Forgive us our debts, as we also have forgiven our debtors.
Matthew 6:12

Jesus referred not to eternal forgiveness but to broken communion with God that is restored by confessing sins daily. When you release your husband from the responsibility to meet all your needs, you will have less to forgive because you then look to the Lord to meet your needs! View forgiveness as a tool God can use to help you become more Christlike.

5. Forgiveness usually includes reconciliation.

A young woman in our community was brutally raped and murdered. The perpetrator was arrested, convicted of the crime, and sent to prison. For years the victim's mother harbored anger and bitterness in her heart towards this man who had taken her daughter's life. After a time, God convicted her of the need to forgive this man. She recognized her own sin and was eventually able to forgive him. Then she wrote to him in prison and shared her change of heart. God continued to impress upon her the need to go to the prison and visit the man face-to-face.

Later, a Christian man speaking to the inmates in a chapel service looked out into the audience and saw the young murderer. Beside him sat his victim's mother. In the prisoner's hands was a Bible with the inscription, "To my son..." That example of forgiveness pales into insignificance many of the issues we hold against others. It also points to our need to reconcile with the offender when doing so does not jeopardize our safety or the safety of others.

Spend the remainder of your time today thanking God for how He has forgiven you and then ask the Lord to show you daily those you need to forgive. If there is anger, hatred, the desire for revenge, or physical attack, then we have to deal with ourselves before we can deal with the offense. When we forsake unholy anger and embrace forgiveness, we are free to deal with those who have wronged us. We can confront and correct with love and truthfulness because our motive is reconciliation rather than revenge!

Wives, you dare not say, "I cannot forgive." What you mean is, "I will not forgive." We can choose to disobey God's command; we can refuse to forgive and continue to harbor bitterness and resentment. But we must never say that we don't forgive because it is impossible! God has forgiven us in Christ, and because of Christ and the cross, nothing is impossible! Will you take Jesus as your model of forgiveness?

Dear God, _____

_____

_____

Week Seven
Sexual Fulfillment

During our early parenting years, David and I were conscientious about the responsibility God had given us to train our three wonderful and unique children (Prov. 22:6). We especially wanted to be prepared for the moment when our children would ask us about love, marriage, and reproduction. We discussed how we would handle this subject matter when the time came.

Jonathan, our oldest, asked questions about sexual love a little bit at a time for several years. David provided just enough information to answer the specific question without volunteering unrequested information.

When he was 10 years old, Jonathan asked David a question so specific that it had to be answered in complete detail. Jonathan sat there with his mouth open gathering in this information. Having lived most of his life in rural Philippines, he had witnessed a lot of procreation in the animal kingdom. But he was entirely unprepared to know how humans reproduced. Somehow, he thought it would be different with us.

David wanted Jonathan to know how fortunate he was to have a Christian parent tell him about God's plan for sexual love. He concluded this teaching moment with the statement, "Jonathan, you know most kids don't get to hear this from their parents."

Jonathan quickly replied, "Yeah, they are really lucky!"

Perhaps, like Jonathan, you have mixed feelings about our studying this topic. If so, you are in good company. I have talked to hundreds of women over the years of my ministry, and very few received a biblical or Christian introduction to sexuality. As a result, they often have false ideas or myths about sexuality in general and the role of sex in marriage.

A marriage characterized by intimacy in the fullest sense must continually confront the world's ideas about sexuality. Satan promotes a view of love that leaves God out of the picture. We must have biblical answers.

This week you will learn that

- God created sexual intimacy to last a lifetime;
- sexual intimacy is exclusive to marriage;
- marriage partners are to fulfill each other sexually;
- we should look for ways to build sexual intimacy in marriage;
- although sex is often misused, we can practice forgiveness and restore our marriage relationships.

This week we will explore God's plan for sexual intimacy within marriage. This plan includes intimacy for a lifetime! May God richly bless you and your husband this week as you study God's design for sexual expressions of love.

Day 1

Created for Your Enjoyment

For this reason ... they will become one flesh. Genesis 2:24

At a conference where I was speaking about sexual intimacy, a woman in her 80s came up to talk to me after the session. All excited and bubbly, she expressed appreciation for everything I said and told me, "You know, my husband and I still enjoy each other intimately! I am so thankful to God that we still have fun! ... It just takes a little longer!"

Wow! I thought, *I want to be like her when I reach her age!* In fact, many younger women don't have the enjoyment and the excitement that this older woman expressed. If you are in a marriage that has lost its sexual excitement, or if your marriage could use a booster shot, the Bible has much to say on this subject. God has the only truth. Unfortunately, much of what people think comes from other sources. In most cases what we hear from the world about sexual love distorts what God created, for Satan can't create; he can only pervert what God has made.

According to Colossians 3:5, underline what are we to do with worldly ideas about sexuality.

Put to death, therefore, whatever belongs to your earthly nature: sexual immorality, impurity, lust, evil desires and greed, which is idolatry. Colossians 3:5

Misconceptions about Sexuality

If we are going to "put to death" unwholesome ideas about sexuality, we must begin by identifying what to discard. Here are some of the misconceptions about sex that often keep women from experiencing it as a wonderful gift from God.

1. Sex is dirty and should not be discussed.

Probably the majority of us grew up in homes where much about sex was left unsaid; you had to fill in the gaps with what your friends said or what the world taught you. If your mother was silent on the subject, you may have concluded that sex is dirty and not to be discussed. Is this true? Not if you read the Bible! At the very beginning of the Bible we read the story of God's plan for sexual procreation and sexual expression of love. Sexuality—both positive and negative—appears throughout the Bible. Obviously, God wanted the home and church to teach about sexuality.

2. Sex is a duty to be performed.

I once talked to a mom and her soon-to-be-married daughter. The daughter asked, "What about the first night? I'm not sure if I'm ready."

Her mother quickly replied, "It's just something you have to do! I was scared the first night, and it was even worse than I could have imagined!"

Is it true that sex is something awful to be dreaded? Is it just a duty you have to perform? Emphatically not! I told the daughter that sexual love is a wonderfully positive experience and something she would enjoy for the rest of her life. I went on to tell her that my husband and I enjoyed a fulfilling sex life. (Sometimes people are surprised to hear this from a pastor's wife!)

3. Sex is impure and perverted.

Many women have experienced sexual abuse, and the entire subject of sex implies impure actions and perversion for them. We can readily understand how an abused person could come to this conclusion, but for real healing to take place, she must confront false beliefs and allow God's healing power and truth to transform her thoughts and emotions.

4. Sex is only for reproduction.

Some were taught that sex is only for the purpose of bringing children into the world. Does the Bible teach that sex, except for the sake of procreation, is impure? No! The Bible says marriage should be honored by all (Heb. 13:4). Furthermore, the Bible discourages marriage partners from sexual abstinence (1 Cor. 7:1-5). Song of Solomon as a whole celebrates romantic love, including pleasurable sexual expressions.

5. Sexual enjoyment is found outside of marriage.

Others find themselves believing that sex is enjoyable only in affairs. After all, that's the way it happens in the movies! I counseled a dear friend who poured her heart out to me because of her husband's affair. Her pain was much more intense because she had seen her father hurt her mother in the same way.

Her mother suffered in silence, but the pain and anger permeated the house. She saw the lack of joy and love her parents showed each other. In contrast, she saw the excitement that her father had for someone else.

Do you not know that he who unites himself with a prostitute is one with her in body? For it is said, "The two will become one flesh."
1 Corinthians 6:16

 Is it true that relationships outside of marriage bring sexual fulfillment? Definitely not! God planned for the marriage relationship to achieve a unique oneness. Read I Corinthians 6:16. How does sex outside of marriage violate God's design?

_____

6. Sex is just a bodily function.

Still others have the idea that sex has nothing to do with actual love—it's just a bodily function. Sex is like eating, drinking, or sleeping. Their sexual partner doesn't matter. In schools today, sex education is often taught as a biological process. Condoms are an option for preventing pregnancy, and abortion is the solution if pregnancy occurs. These courses never mention the emotional wounds laid bare in sexual relationships—and women are so emotionally vulnerable. They never describe the pain and hurt that failed relationships bring. Unfortunately, they rarely teach about the pure joy and satisfaction that can come from loving one person for a lifetime.

The Influence of Our Families

Once we have examined the misconceptions about sex that are so prevalent in our world today, we should ask ourselves how and why some of these attitudes have crept into our thinking.

 The following questions will help you to determine your own sexual beliefs and attitudes. First, how and from whom did you first hear about sex? What was your reaction?

_____

How did your parents deal with sexual issues? How did their approach influence your opinions regarding sex?

_____

What influences as a young child colored your sexual attitudes?

_____

_____

How does your style of dealing with your children about sexuality differ from your parents' style of dealing with you?

_____

_____

Childhood attitudes and experiences don't have to determine forever our sexuality, for God has given us the mind of Christ (see I Cor. 2:16). He can change our thoughts, actions, and attitudes! Now we will examine biblical principles that should govern our sexual attitudes and behaviors.

God's Plan

Some have argued that sexual intimacy must have been created after the fall of man, but we know clearly from the Scriptures that God created intimacy in marriage before sin entered the world in Genesis 3:6.

Read Genesis 1:28,31 and 2:24. What was God's opinion of male and female?

☐ unclean   ☐ necessary evil   ☐ very good

What did God mean by "they will become one flesh" (2:24)?

_____

God blessed them and said to them, "Be fruitful and increase in number; fill the earth and subdue it. Rule over the fish of the sea and the birds of the air and over every living creature that moves on the ground."
Genesis 1:28

God saw all that he had made, and it was very good.
Genesis 1:31

A man will leave his father and mother and be united to his wife, and they will become one flesh.
Genesis 2:24

God Himself is the Author and Creator of sexual intimacy. When God created the woman, Adam announced to the world, "This is now bone of my bones and flesh of my flesh. She shall be called woman for she was taken out of man" (Gen. 2:23). We should value our physical bodies as a creation of the Master Designer, made just the way God intended.

We should be careful not to call what God created bad or wrong, when He stated that all that He had made was very good, then blessed the one man-one woman relationship. If you have identified an issue today that needs re-thinking, will you allow Christ to adjust your thinking? Pray for the "mind of Christ" in this matter.

Dear God, _____

_____

_____

Day 2

Marriage: Sexually Exclusive

Marriage should be honored by all, and the marriage bed kept pure.
Hebrews 13:4

A little girl asked her grandmother, "Grandma, how old are you?"

The grandmother replied, "Now dear, you shouldn't ask that question. Most grown-ups don't like to tell their age."

The following day, the girl had another question. "Grandma, how much do you weigh?"

Once again the grandmother replied, "Oh, honey, you shouldn't ask grown-ups how much they weigh. It isn't polite."

The next day the little girl had a big smile on her face. She said, "Grandma, you're 62, and you weigh 140 pounds."

The grandmother was surprised. "My goodness, how did you know?"

The girl smiled and said, "You left your driver's license on the table, and I read it. I also saw on your license that you flunked sex."

Would you and I flunk God's test on sexuality? A friend of mine taught the parents and teenagers in our church about God's plan for sex. In the opening session, she gave a test to each group. She discovered that the parents knew less than the teenagers.

We seldom think of God and sex together. We see God as holy, but is sex holy? The world tries to separate sexuality from spirituality. Even the church has struggled through the centuries with the connection between the two. As a result, the world views Christians as negative or naive.

In my own Christian upbringing, sex was little talked about at church. As a youth, we were told it was wrong, but nothing was mentioned about the joy of marital intimacy. Because our parents and the church were silent or negative about the subject of sex, we were left to struggle on our own for a healthy and biblical view of human sexuality.

Sexual Imagery in the Bible

In the Old Testament when Israel was far from God, she was continually called a "prostitute" (Jer. 2:20). She had left her first love and gone after anything else her heart desired.

In 2 Corinthians 11:2, Paul wrote, "I promised you to one husband, to Christ, so that I might present you as a pure virgin to him." The sexual union in the covenant of marriage is compared to the "oneness" God desires with His people. Not only did God ordain the oneness between husband and wife, but He honored this relationship. It pictured to the world the relationship between God and His people!

 Read Ephesians 5:31-32. Paraphrase the "profound mystery."

_____

"A man will leave his father and mother and be united to his wife, and the two will become one flesh." This is a profound mystery—but I am talking about Christ and the church.
Ephesians 5:31-32

In the New Testament, the church is called the bride of Christ (see Rev. 21:2). Because marriage pictures the relationship between Jesus and His bride (those who have a saving relationship with Christ), we must take seriously the image we present of marriage. Others who look at our marriages will see Christ in our picture, or they will not see Him at all.

Sexual oneness is exclusive to marriage.

 Read Proverbs 5:15-23 in your Bible. Paraphrase Solomon's warning.

_____

_____

Solomon warned the young man not to waste or share his sexual attention with strangers. He was to be only with the wife of his youth—his first wife. A sexual liaison outside of marriage dishonors what God created as pure and refreshing. Much heartache results when we disregard God's plan.

In I Corinthians 6:15-20, our relationship of oneness with God through Christ is compared to the oneness of a sexually intimate couple. When you are united sexually, you become one with the other person. Clearly, oneness is intended only within marriage.

Paul wrote this letter to the Corinthian people who had lived immorally before they became Christians. They worshiped Aphrodite, the goddess of love, and during this time more than one thousand temple prostitutes served in the temple. The expression *to Corinthianize* came to mean practicing sexual immorality. When the Corinthian believers came to know Jesus Christ as their Lord and Savior, they had much to learn about God's intentions when He created sexual beings.

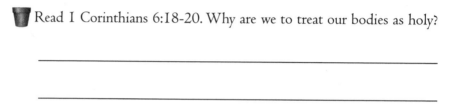 Read I Corinthians 6:18-20. Why are we to treat our bodies as holy?

_____

_____

Flee from sexual immorality. All other sins a man commits are outside his body, but he who sins sexually sins against his own body. Do you not know that your body is a temple of the Holy Spirit, who is in you, whom you have received from God? You are not your own; you were bought at a price. Therefore honor God with your body.
1 Corinthians 6:18-20

Paul clearly stated that sexual immorality is a sin against our bodies, which are the temple of the Holy Spirit. Paul urged the Corinthian believers to flee sexual immorality—that means run from it!

What is at stake?

Our world is not much different from Corinth during Paul's day. Sexual infidelity and immorality are widespread. Satan has used the lust of the flesh to damage human society. When God's plan is not followed, pain and misery result. "The wages of sin is death" (Rom. 6:23).

Have you ever been given a gift and then the giver asked for it back? I can remember each of my children doing just that. The first time it caught me by surprise, but after that my pre-birthday party instructions always included, "Now remember this is for your friend, and you are so happy to give this to him (her). Now don't ask for this back because it is theirs, not yours!" Despite my good instructions, we left a few parties in tears and even caused a few tears.

Receiving gifts can be one of the greatest joys in life. No matter how old we are, when something is taken away from us that was previously given willingly, it hurts! When we come into marriage, we promise to love and cherish our husbands above all others. If that love is taken back, the pain is indescribable. Infidelity hurts to the core of our being.

Christians have much at stake in the spiritual battle for sexual purity. Sex has great power. God designed it for our enjoyment; therefore, it is intended to have much appeal. When sexuality is abused, devastating consequences follow. Unlike some other sins, sexual sin is inseparably tied to our emotions, our identities, and our spirituality. No matter how casual sex is intended to be, physical union is always a binding of two into one (see I Cor. 6). If the two are then separated back into separate individuals and go their own ways, pain always results. Many Christians believe that infidelity is the most significant violation of an agreement of trust that can ever affect them.

We will discuss the pain of infidelity in day 5. Only God can heal such a wound. If you have been tempted by sexual pleasures outside of marriage, ask God for a pure heart and mind. If you have been withholding sexual love from your marriage—other than for a time on which you and your husband have mutually agreed—confess this sin as well.

Dear God, _____

_____

_____

Day 3
Sexual Satisfaction

The husband should fulfill his marital duty to his wife, and likewise the wife to her husband. 1 Corinthians 7:3

We cannot separate the intimate relationship we have with our husbands from our relationship with God. It pictures or mirrors the relationship between Christ and the church. If we are walking in obedience to the Lord, naturally we'll want our marriage relationships to bring honor and glory to Him. We'll want to love our husbands the way God intended.

Have you noticed a connection between the vitality of your walk with God and the sexual temperature in your bedroom? Explain how the two might be related.

_____

_____

Partners are to fulfill each other sexually.

In the Proverbs 5:15-23 passage we read in day 2, Solomon clearly intended for the young man to rejoice and be thankful for his wife's sexuality. She provided sexual satisfaction; he had no reason to look beyond this relationship. In fact, he was captivated by her love.

 Read I Corinthians 7:1-5 in your Bible. What is the Christian wife's

responsibility to her husband? _____

_____

Men and women differ in their sexual responses and physiology, but they should both view their bodies as belonging to their mates. Both are to receive sexual pleasure and satisfaction from physical union. We have a responsibility to meet the sexual needs of our husbands so they will know they are loved, appreciated, and accepted.

You may be saying, *But Lana, my marriage does not bring me sexual satisfaction.* We will address this problem in day 4. Let me remind you that the solution is not abstaining from sex. Paul emphatically states that this approach is not a workable solution in marriage (I Cor. 7:5).

Intimacy in marriage is not to be interrupted except on very rare occasions. The healthy, God-given drive of a husband and wife is not to be restrained, restricted, or squelched no matter how long they have been married except for three basic reasons.

 According to I Corinthians 7:5, when is it permissible for a husband and wife to sexually abstain?

_____

Stop depriving one another, except by agreement for a time that you may devote yourselves to prayer, and come together again lest Satan tempt you because of your lack of self-control."
1 Corinthians 7:5, NASB

We are not to deprive our husbands except by mutual agreement. Agreement requires discussion. I am greatly concerned about the attitude of some Christian wives. They may discuss every other aspect of their relationships with their husbands, but not sexual intimacy. They expect their spouses to read their minds about their sexual desires. Then they use depriving them as manipulation to get their way or as a way to strike back at them for something they did or failed to do. This should not be.

We are to abstain only when there is a focused need for prayer. These are times when our usual prayer life seems inadequate. We feel a need for concerted prayer, often including fasting. Our total focus is on God.

When David and I lost our fourth child, we were numb with pain. We mutually agreed to abstain from sex. We spent time with the Lord and focused on the healing of our emotions. We came back together very shortly because the intimacy and oneness that we experienced sexually was also God's plan for healing us. We drew comfort from each other.

The child of King David and Bathsheba was ill and at the point of death. In 2 Samuel 12:16 David fasted and prayed. The servant and elders of his household saw his pain. When the child died, David spent time in worship and then arose and went to Bathsheba.

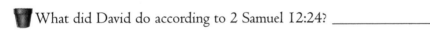 What did David do according to 2 Samuel 12:24? _____

_____

David comforted his wife Bathsheba, and he went to her and lay with her.
2 Samuel 12:24

David comforted his wife. They were one together in their pain, bodies, and hearts. Sexual intimacy can bring healing to a relationship. It expresses emotions that no words can. It represents being there for your husband. It communicates love, acceptance, and value.

Abstaining from sexual intimacy is to be temporary. Limiting the time lessens Satan's ability to tempt us. When we deprive our husbands, we help Satan open the door to temptation. We build barriers that will prevent continued intimacy and growth in the relationship.

Developing a healthy sex life doesn't guarantee fidelity in marriage, but it promotes it. If your husband has been sexually unfaithful, don't jump to the conclusion that you weren't sexually responsive. No one can stand before God and say, "She made me do it." We are accountable for our own actions. Many women have needlessly and inaccurately blamed themselves for their husbands' affairs. At the same time, we want to promote faithfulness.

Sexual union should honor and glorify God.

 Read Hebrews 13:4 (see page 142). Does sex within marriage bring honor and glory to God? (circle) yes no

The marriage bed is pure; adultery is what brings defilement. God will judge the adulterer and all the sexually immoral, but what is done in the marriage bed is to be unstained by the world; it is to be honored. God wants all that we do with our bodies to bring glory and honor to Him.

Why do men and women enter into extramarital experiences? Studies have shown that women tend to be motivated by their emotional needs of being loved, accepted, and appreciated. Men initially are motivated by their physical needs, but then the affair can develop into a very emotional experience. God's manual for sexual expression is the only true and lasting guide for sexual satisfaction.

Marriage partners differ from each other.

How are men and women different physically? Men are sexually aroused by visual stimulation. Understanding this fact helps us recognize that sexual intimacy within marriage will not be facilitated by going to bed in rollers or wearing a facial mask. We want to look attractive to our husbands, since God created them to respond visually.

 Rate your usual night-time appearance as you climb into bed.

●————————————————————————————————●

a bad dream   a vision of loveliness

Women are primarily excited by the sense of touch. Let your husband know the areas of your body and types of touches that you find stimulating. Women are also influenced by their menstrual calendar. Share with your husband the times each month you are more desirous of him.

Women are also excited by the romantic aura which surrounds the experience. In other words, if her husband spends time in intimacy talking, a woman is more likely to desire intimacy. His character and personality greatly affect her sexual feelings for him. For the woman, sex is an emotional experience which begins in the mind. In other words, if a husband spends time in intimacy talking (romantic words, compliments, pleasurable memories, and so forth) then a woman is more likely to desire intimacy.

A woman who refuses or hesitates to meet her husband's sexual needs puts him in a vulnerable situation. When he enters marriage, he promises to remain faithful "until death do us part." This commitment indicates he trusts his wife to be as sexually interested in him as he is in her. When a wife withholds herself from her husband, she fails to meet his physical needs. She also damages his self-esteem. A man needs to know that his wife enjoys him sexually as much as he enjoys her. When there is only sexual release without her enjoyment, his needs are only partially met.

 Have you been selfish in your approach to lovemaking?
(circle) yes no

Today will you ask the Lord to show you ways to build sexual intimacy in your marriage? How can you better meet your husband's sexual needs? Give your relationship with your husband to the Lord.

Dear God, _____

_____

_____

Day 4
The Song of Solomon on Sex

Place me like a seal over your heart, like a seal on your arm;
for love is as strong as death. Song of Solomon 8:6

The Bible is a marvelous handbook on intimacy. Today we will be reading from the Song of Songs, and if this is your first time to read this book, you are in for a surprise! This song was written by King Solomon, the son of David and Bathsheba. It describes love in all its beauty and excitement as a gift from God.

God intends that sexual love between a husband and wife, with all its passion and spontaneity, be experienced as a normal part of marital life. In this book we find some practical suggestions for how to build this love in our lives. Recall my promise from day 3. If you will practice the intimacy-building principles taken from the Song of Solomon, you will increase the likelihood of sexual satisfaction in your marriage.

In this song of love the voice of the beloved, a female voice, is dominant. This song begins, "Let him kiss me with the kisses of his mouth—for your love is more delightful than wine" (v. 2). It ends with a beckon to come away with her and partake of this gift of love (8:14).

When Solomon speaks, he is referred to as the lover. The lover and the beloved have a beautiful relationship that is noticed by others, mentioned in the book as friends.

 Now, find a comfortable chair, have your highlighter pen in hand, and read all 8 chapters in the Song of Solomon. Keep in mind the following questions as you read.
1. How did they physically express their love?
2. How did they verbally express their love through compliments?
3. What different things did they share with each other?

Affirmation builds intimacy.

 How does the beloved describe herself in 1:5-6? Check one.

☐ dark-skinned　　☐ like a tent　　☐ a sun-worshiper

How does Solomon describe her in 1:15? _____

How does the beloved describe Solomon in 1:16? _____

_____

The beloved was dark, deeply browned by the sun. At this time, bronzed skin was undesirable because it was gained not in a tanning salon but out in the fields and vineyards while laboring long hours. However, Solomon declared his beloved beautiful! When we build up the one we love with words of affirmation, we enhance that person's self-image. Your words can elevate how your husband feels about himself.

Apples and raisins were common symbols of love in the Middle East. How does the beloved compliment Solomon in 2:3-5?

_____

The beloved not only affirmed her lover with her words, but she declared him to be a wonderful lover! Every man has a desire to be a great lover, and in fact, his ego is tied to his ability in this area. A man is not completely fulfilled if only he has gotten release; he needs for his wife to also enjoy their relationship. Ladies, we must show our husbands that we desire them and that we enjoy being intimate with them. One of the best ways to show that you think your husband is a wonderful lover is through your words. Throughout the Song of Songs, the beloved expressed how well her lover demonstrated his love for her.

Read Song of Solomon 3:1-4; 4:16. Describe what the beloved did to let Solomon know that she desired him.

_____

_____

She searched for him and declared that he was the one her heart desired. When she found him, she wouldn't let him go! The beloved invited him to come into her garden, which represents love's intimacies. Ladies, this is absolutely awesome. If you treated your husband in a similar manner, he might not go to work! At least he would be anxious to get home and would think of you all day long. We would do well to cultivate the ability to verbalize our admiration of our husbands.

What are some ways you can affirm your husband as your lover? You will not be asked to share this in your group, so be specific. List these in the margin.

Enjoyment builds intimacy.

Each one admired the other, and they each reached out passionately to the other. They found encouragement, praise, honor, and delight in just being with one another. Not only were they lovers, they were friends. Their thoughts were continually focused on each other. Joy came merely by thinking of the other. How long has it been since the mere thought of your husband created excitement?

The beloved in this passage looks upon her lover's body with expressed pleasure (5:10-15). She totally enjoyed the intimacy that she shared with her lover. Can you imagine what your husband would do if you said these words to him tonight? Maybe your husband would not be confused with a movie star, but look at him through the eyes of love. These eyes aren't blind or naive, but they see the best in a person. In Song of Solomon 7:1-9, the husband also views his wife with pleasure. In this reciprocal relationship, both verbally appreciate one another and show their love and preference in tangible ways.

The climax of this book is found in chapter 8, verses 6-7. In your own words describe what these verses teach about love.

_____

_____

Place me like a seal over
your heart,
like a seal on your arm;
for love is as strong as death,
its jealousy unyielding
as the grave.
It burns like blazing fire,
like a mighty flame.
Many waters cannot
quench love;
rivers cannot wash
it away.
It one were to give
all the wealth of his
house for love
it would be utterly scorned.
Song of Songs 8:6-7

Young Jewish men were not permitted to read this book until they reached the age of Jewish adulthood. Why? Because this book describes the beauty of an intimate relationship between lovers. These verses characterize love as the strongest, most unyielding and invincible force in the human experience.

Communication builds intimacy.

One of the reasons the beloved and the lover were able to share and give freely was their ability to verbally express what they needed and desired. When they enjoyed how the other one made them feel physically, they were able to express this thought.

When the beloved requested raisins and apples (2:5), she was saying that she was sick or weak with love. She requested that her lover come and caress her. Then in 2:6, she described the position they were in while they were carrying on a conversation with each other.

Many husbands and wives have no idea what pleases the other because they are having silent sex. It is OK to talk during lovemaking; in fact, it will build and strengthen your enjoyment of each other. How can we know what brings the most pleasure unless we ask?

Excuses undermine intimacy.

In chapter 5 the lover knocked at her door late at night. What was the beloved's reply to his knock (5:3)?

☐ she quickly opened the door   ☐ she made excuses
☐ she suggested he come another time

She complained that she couldn't get up because she would have to put on her robe and wash her feet again! We can delay lovemaking with many excuses, such as the famous one, "I've got a headache." Do not try to camouflage an excuse as a legitimate reason for postponement.

What excuses have you used? List these in the margin.

What did Solomon do after she made excuses (5:6)?

☐ he beat the door down   ☐ he left   ☐ he slept on her porch

Excuses dishonor God's plan and affect our relationship with Him. We must put away our excuses and come together as one as God intended.

Focusing our thoughts builds intimacy.

In Song of Songs 5:10-16 Solomon's beloved described her lover physically. She thought about his positive attributes, his character, and his physical appearance. Her thoughts were focused on their life together.

If your thoughts are on someone beside your husband, will you discipline them and bring them into captivity to Christ? He can transform your thinking, change your desires, and give you the freedom to love and to receive love as you have never before experienced it! Ask Him.

I have taken off my robe—
must I put it on again?
I have washed my feet—
must I soil them again?
Song of Songs 5:3

I opened for my lover,
but my lover had left;
he was gone.
My heart sank at
his departure.
I looked for him but did
not find him.
I called him but he did
not answer.
Song of Songs 5:6

Four Ways to Build Intimacy
1. Practice affirmation.
2. Enjoy each other.
3. Avoid excuses.
4. Focus your thoughts.

Day 5
Situations That Affect Intimacy

Call upon me in the day of trouble; I will deliver you. Psalm 50:15

Today we want to focus on what we can do about situations that affect sexual intimacy with our husbands. Although it is a difficult subject, I believe we must deal with hearts that are broken by sexual abuse, infidelity, and other misuses of sex. Many of you fail to experience the sexual intimacy God designed for your marriage because of a horrible wrong committed against you. Some of you may harbor anger and bitterness towards your husband, which inhibits sexual intimacy. You may find yourself detesting sexual intimacy and aren't really sure why.

Through our study today, I pray each of you will experience emotional healing and then live in the joy of the Lord. Let's meet two women (whose names have been changed) I have counseled personally.

Cathy's Story

Cathy grew up in a home where she was sexually abused at a young age by her uncle. The abuse continued into her teenage years. She withdrew from all of her friends, both male and female, putting up such a barrier around herself that no one could get in.

While in college, Cathy met a fellow student named Tim. For the first time, she felt the freedom to talk to someone, and she felt safe. Through his Christian testimony, she embraced Jesus Christ, and the process of emotional healing began. Cathy's friendship with Tim blossomed into love, and he asked her to marry him.

As they made plans for their wedding, Cathy started retreating back into her shell, where no one could hurt her. Tim tried every means possible to reach her, but Cathy was filled with irrational fear. Although she knew she could trust Tim and had no doubts at all about her love for him, the fear of sexual intimacy overwhelmed her.

Cathy married Tim, but from the beginning, sexual intimacy was frightful. Over time and daily dependence on God, she realized that God designed sexual intimacy to be good and that Satan had perverted it. With Tim's patience and unconditional love, Cathy accepted intimacy as a gift from God and gave Him all her fears. Tim and Cathy still have problems, but they have begun to experience joy in their intimate sexual relationship together.

Valerie's Story

Valerie found out while she was pregnant that her husband was in a long-term affair. Her feelings ranged from deep hurt to desperation. At work, she functioned mechanically. She didn't see how she could continue with her pregnancy and tried three times unsuccessfully to terminate it.

She pleaded for her husband to call off the affair; she spewed anger at him, but he remained unmoved and unrepentant. Eventually, she asked him to leave the house. She was hospitalized, her life in shambles.

Valerie, who had faith in God, then began the long process of healing her anger and bitterness by beginning an intensive study of God's Word. She read Christian books and talked to a Christian counselor. God showed her the way of forgiveness and restoration of her heart. She now lives an abundant life, full of joy and hope, and reaches out to others in her same situation. God has used her greatly.

Typical Reactions

Both Cathy and Valerie faced difficult choices in dealing with their different experiences. Their choices determined the extent of their peace and joy. J. Allen Peterson lists five of the most common responses that occur when sex has been misused.[1]

1. **The Freeze Reaction**—denying the evidence that the hurt (affair, abuse …) is real. This refusal to confront allows the hurt to deepen.
2. **The Fry Reaction**—feeling righteous indignation and self-pity. The person has been wounded and is very angry.
3. **The Fold Reaction**—personalizing the situation and taking all the blame. He or she dwells on past mistakes.
4. **The Fight Reaction**—looking for ways to punish the spouse and anyone else who may be involved.
5. **The Force Reaction**—pushing hard for an immediate solution; manipulating the people involved for a quick fix.

Unfortunately, none of these reactions brings back the joy or reconciles the relationship. How do we deal with the feelings that result because our trust has been destroyed?

Hosea's Story

In the Bible the prophet Hosea struggled with his wife's infidelity. Frequently described as the broken prophet of tears, Hosea was able to restore his marriage and the intimacy that God intended. The book of Hosea also pictures how God reached out to the people of Israel who were playing the harlot by worshipping other gods and rejecting their true Father. We can learn from Hosea's response.

In Hosea 2:2 what is Hosea's plea? _____

_____

"Let her remove the adulterous look from her face and the unfaithfulness from between her breasts."
Hosea 2:2

155

Despite the natural tendency to withdraw from a spouse who is unfaithful, Hosea appealed to his wife to cease her affair. Hosea's response teaches us to face the problem and not to avoid the issue. This is really the most difficult step, for you must deal with the problem while you are broken. We find it so much easier to retreat and pretend that nothing has happened.

Others prefer to focus on the injustice and their right to be angry. It is not unusual to experience the Freeze, the Fry, or the Fight Reaction as described above. This is a time to make a conscious decision to keep the door of communication open, even though the hurt is great.

Instead, speaking the truth in love, we will in all things grow up into him who is the Head, that is, Christ.
Ephesians 4:15

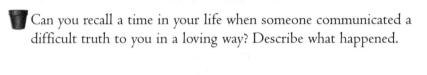 Underline the type of communication we are to have according to Ephesians 4:15.

Speaking the truth in a loving manner is very difficult when our hearts are broken. It is much easier to speak the truth about the injustice done. At the other extreme is the wife who speaks sweet words but hides the real truth about her feelings. She may not want to rock the boat, but the truth stays bottled up inside and can result in depression. I have found that one of the best ways to communicate in love is to share how I am feeling without casting blame or prejudging the other person.

Can you recall a time in your life when someone communicated a difficult truth to you in a loving way? Describe what happened.

_____

_____

Ephesians 4:26-32 tells us to express anger appropriately. We are not to deny the hurt, but at the same time, we are not to lash out. Avoid uncontrolled temper, insults, sharp criticism, or arguing for the sake of arguing. Our words should build up, not tear down.

As I say this, I know how difficult emotional control is at a time of deep woundedness. Hurt can be overwhelming; only through the power of the Holy Spirit can we speak the truth in love and express our anger in a way that would bring glory to God!

I know in my own strength I can't do this. Only God's love working in me can overcome tough situations such as we have been describing.

When you find yourself in this situation, pray—for yourself, for your husband, and for anyone else who has sinned against you.

If praying about your situation does not bring reconciliation, I strongly urge you to get godly counsel through your church or a Christian counselor. Two persons must be willing to work together to repair a damaged relationship.

■ What was Hosea's desire for Gomer in Hosea 2:6-7? _____

_____

Hosea desired that she would hunger for what God intended and find unsatisfying what the world had to offer. He yearned that she would realize that only God's good and perfect will brings true satisfaction. When your partner is caught in the web of infidelity, pray for him. Pray that he will not find satisfaction and that his unsatisfied hunger will be so great that he will seek God.

In Hosea 2:9-13 we read the bitter consequences for the unfaithful: the "new wine," the joy of the love that God has given, will not be experienced. Pray that God will show your husband the joy of his first love and the joy of living in obedience to God.

God told Hosea to show his love to the wife who was unfaithful. He pointed out that He loves the unfaithful in this same way. Christ bought us with His crucifixion on the cross, just as Hosea was instructed to buy back his wife (Hos. 3:2).

Ladies, I am brought to tears when I think of how many times I have rejected God's love by my disobedience and rebellion. How can I not give another chance to those who have failed me? How can I not show others the same love that God has showed me?

■ We each choose our response to the hurt we have experienced at the hands of someone else. Is there a hurt you need to give to the Lord? As you write, be aware of times you have hurt the heart of God.

_____

It may be that you are not aware of an injustice done against you, but you remain choked with feelings that inhibit sexual intimacy. Perhaps selfishness has put a barrier between you and your husband. Maybe

Therefore I will block her path with thornbushes; I will wall her in so that she cannot find her way. She will chase after her lovers but not catch them; she will look for them but not find them. Then she will say, 'I will go back to my husband as at first, for then I was better off than now.'
Hosea 2:6-7

hurtful words, pride, or any number of small things have happened. You may have rejected your husband's overtures of intimacy so many times that he does not make them anymore. Anger and resentment may have built up to the point where you cannot even stand to be touched.

The material shared this week on sexual intimacy has undoubtedly pointed out many failures for each of us. What are we to do? Whatever has happened, forgiveness can be found at the feet of Jesus. First John 1:9-10 promises forgiveness for all who confess their sins openly and honestly to God. Avoid the error of noting all your spouse's failings; you can't confess the sins of another. Begin with your own mistakes.

 Circle *Y* for yes, *S* for sometimes, or *N* for no, indicating the appropriate response for each question.

- Have I viewed sexual intimacy as a curse rather than the gift of God? Y S N
- Have I been selfish in my attitude toward sex? Y S N
- Have I deprived my husband of sex to punish him? Y S N
- Have I entertained impure thoughts? Y S N
- Have I been "too busy" for my husband? (Maybe even too busy serving the Lord?) Y S N
- Have I failed to express unconditional love to my husband? Y S N
- Have I given a false report to my children on the subject of sex? Y S N
- Have I tried to leave God out of my sexual relations with my husband? Y S N

Review the list, and let the Holy Spirit search your heart. Now, make plans to change your actions as well as your attitudes. Has sexual intimacy in your marriage fallen into a rut? Make a list of some things you can do to rebuild intimacy in your marriage. It could be as simple as a short love note or a mini-moon (short honeymoon).

Today, will you make the choice to be "captivated" by the love of your husband? Commit your marriage to the Lord and ask Him for the fullness of His design for you and your husband.

---

[1]J. Allan Petersen, *The Myth of the Greener Grass* (Wheaton: Tyndale House Publishers, Inc., 1983), 103–18.

Covenant Commitment

On her 50th wedding anniversary a wife was asked how her marriage had lasted so long. "When we got married," she replied, "we didn't know you could quit." Commitment to marriage has become *passé.* Instead of "till death do us part," our culture has changed the words to "till disagreements do us part" or "till other interests do us part." Marriage lasts as long as both parties feel like it or until they get tired of each other. This attitude is contrary to God's original plan.

I heard a story about a young man who wanted a duplicate of his girlfriend's picture, so he took it to the photographer. As the photographer took it out of the frame, he noticed the inscription on the back: "I'll love you forever … P.S. I want this picture back if we break up." Sadly, even as the relationship began, the girlfriend already had a contingency plan for the break up.

Quitting the marriage is an all too quick first response for those experiencing difficulties. Christians are not exempt. Studies show the divorce rate for Christians is equal to the secular world's rate. Because Christians have the help and power from God available to us, quitting should not be our initial response to domestic problems.

Oh ladies, God wants to show His lavish lovingkindness to you, your marriages, and your families. That doesn't mean we won't face the difficulties the world faces. Because of sin, God's perfect plan was marred. But at the very beginning God provided the super abundance of His resources and power to us if we will just ask and seek Him.

In the past weeks we have studied our roles as women and wives. We have examined our hearts and our relationship with God. We have focused on God's original plan in Genesis 2, which fills us with hope. This week, we will affirm commitment to our marriages while at the same time dealing with issues in troubled marriages.

This week you will learn that

- as a member of God's royal priesthood, you can take your concerns to God directly;
- God's unquestionable goodness gives us assurance that He hears our requests;
- Jesus taught marriage for a lifetime;
- God is in the business of miracles, and He wants to bless your marriage relationship;
- commitment in marriage requires a committed heart.

Day 1

A Reason to Keep Trying

Cast your cares on the Lord and he will sustain you; he will never let the righteous fall. Psalm 55:22

"I just don't love him anymore. We were just children when we got married. Don't tell me about God. I have taught classes about God, and I have served Him faithfully. I've tried to be the best wife and mother possible, but I can't get back my feelings for my husband."

"If only you knew the frustrations that I have had in my marriage. I've put myself aside and met the needs of everyone else. I need to be with someone who can love me and make me feel special. I've met this man … He accepts me. I can relax with him. We haven't slept together, but I just can't go on with my husband."

What would you say to someone who came to you and poured out these feelings? How do you think this person would respond to your sharing the belief that marriage is for a lifetime? How would she respond to insights you have learned from this study?

She'd probably shake her head and say, "I've tried! Sounds good—but I am tired of being the only one who changes." Encouragement to be a godly wife would possibly be met with deaf ears.

Recently I talked to a lady I admire very much. She had persevered in a marriage with a husband who was caught up in a long-term affair. She had spent years being a good wife, yet her husband had not changed and was continuing his affair. She came to the point where she asked, "Is there really any need to continue trying? Doesn't this problem warrant despair?"

The real question that each of these ladies asked was not, "What should I do?" but rather "Is there any reason not to despair? Is there any reason at all why I should not see my marriage as a total failure and beyond hope? Is there any reason to keep on trying?" Honestly, haven't we all asked this question at times?

In whom or what do you trust?

These are tough questions, and the answers will not be found with a pat response such as, "Just wait, things will get better if you keep trying." Today we will look at the basis of Christian hope: God's nature and character and not circumstances or the people around us. This hope is not dependent on your husband but based on the grace of God.

God did not promise that our way would be easy, but He did promise that He would be with us through everything. God can use every circumstance. Your responsibility is to respond to life's events in the way that pleases God. Then, you have reason to hope. Hope is bound up in the presence and purposes of God in our lives.

 Read Matthew 26:65. Underline what action Caiaphas took to indicate his displeasure with Jesus' answer.

The context of Matthew 26:65 is Jesus on trial before the high priest before His crucifixion. Jesus had stated clearly who He was, and then Caiaphas, the high priest, tore his robes.

In the Bible people tore their robes as a way of expressing grief and distress. Joshua and Caleb tore their clothes when the Israelites refused to believe in the victory that God could give them in the land of Canaan. Jephythah tore his clothes when his daughter first greeted him after a hasty vow he made that whoever greeted him first after returning from battle would be sacrificed.

Tearing one's clothing was the accepted cultural custom that visually showed a loss of hope and inability to go on in the present circumstances. Have you ever felt if one more thing happened, you would break into pieces from the inside out? This is a very vulnerable time.

 What one person did God specifically command not to tear his clothing according to Leviticus 21:10?

_____

_____

When two of Aaron's sons were killed, what did Moses command Aaron, the high priest not to do in Leviticus 10:6?

_____

_____

The people of Israel were expected to tear their clothes to show their deep emotions and despair. In fact, paid professional mourners tore their clothing and cried on behalf of the family. But Aaron, a priest of God, would have been killed if he had done so! Why were kings and other

The high priest tore his clothes and said, "He has spoken blasphemy! Why do we need any more witnesses? Look, now you have heard the blasphemy."
Matthew 26:65

"'The high priest, the one among his brothers who has had the anointing oil poured on his head and who has been ordained to wear the priestly garments, must not let his hair become unkempt or tear his clothes.'"
Leviticus 21:10

Moses said to Aaron and his sons Eleazar and Ithamar, "Do not let your hair become unkempt, and do not tear your clothes, or you will die and the Lord will be angry with the whole community. But your relatives, all the house of Israel, may mourn for those the Lord has destroyed by fire."
Leviticus 10:6

leaders allowed to tear their clothes and yet the priest was prohibited from tearing his clothes?

The priests served in the tabernacle and enjoyed access to holy places that others could not enter. they were constantly reminded of God—His holiness, His person, His purposes, His glory, His provision. They lived with visual reminders that they had God as their provider and Resource.

When you are aware of God's continual presence in your life, nothing can happen that can take away your hope. God's grace is sufficient for all circumstances. You have direct access to God's power and wisdom.

 Read 1 Peter 2:1-10. What is your position according to 1 Peter 2:5,9?

_____

You also, like living stones, are being built into a spiritual house to be a holy priesthood, offering spiritual sacrifices acceptable to God through Jesus Christ.

You are a chosen people, a royal priesthood, a holy nation, a people belonging to God, that you may declare the praises of him who called you out of darkness into his wonderful light.
1 Peter 2:5,9

We are a holy priesthood with daily access to God. Whenever difficulties arise, we can enter God's presence. We are exhorted to live our lives as priests. What a privilege! I did not always take my concerns directly to God. As a teenager, I would look for a close friend with whom I could work out my feelings. As my walk in Christ matured, I would seek advice from godly people. But a point came when I realized I could go to God with my questions and emotions! He could handle them. He had been waiting all my life for me to trust Him with my vulnerability.

When we are angry, we can cry out to God. When we are hurt, He hears our groans. Our Lord offers consolation, a listening ear, a tender touch, and healing.

Cast your cares on the Lord and he will sustain you; he will never let the righteous fall.
Psalm 55:22

 What does Psalm 55:22 say we are to do with our burdens?

_____

_____

No matter what happens, because we are priests, we can bring our burdens boldly to the throne of God with confidence that He understands our problems and the depth of our struggles. We come knowing that God is faithful and all-powerful and can work through our circumstances for His purposes and His glory. Therefore, since we have this special position and privilege, we are never to tear our robes. We must never see any situation as being so hopeless that there can only be despair.

What do you think keeps us from giving God all our cares?

_____

_____

No Need for Despair

Now let's go back to the question that we asked at the beginning of today's session: "Is there any reason why I shouldn't see my marriage as a total failure and beyond hope? Is there any reason to keep trying?" Are we to tear our clothes by being a living martyr and saying, "I'll just stay with him till death do us part"? Should we rip our garments by escaping through divorce? Are we to cut up our clothes by seeking the companionship of someone else?

No, we don't need to despair because God is waiting and willing to carry all our burdens, even if our husbands will not join in our pursuit of commitment. We have all of God's resources and His Spirit dwelling in us. We don't need to fear what our husbands or others may do.

We can put all our burdens on God because He is trustworthy. No longer do we need to fear "what if" or "what about;" instead, we have the assurance that God is for us (Ps. 56:9). Let those words sink in. God wants the best for you. When you feel all alone, God is there! Just as a small child takes great comfort from his mother putting her gentle hand on his shoulder, we too can take great comfort in God's presence. When you are afraid of the future, God is near. What burdens, fears, circumstances, or people do you need to give to the Lord today?

Be anxious for nothing, but in everything by prayer and supplication with thanksgiving let your requests be made known to God. And the peace of God, which surpasses all comprehension, shall guard your hearts and your minds in Christ Jesus.
Philippians 4:6-7, NASB

Dear God, _____

_____

_____

Day 2

The Reality of God's Goodness

Taste and see that the Lord is good. Psalm 34:8

Do you believe that God's purposes are always good? Then you will earnestly want to follow His plan for your life. Commitment to our marriages should be based on a desire to obey God because we know He is good! If God is for you, who can be against you (Rom. 8:31)?

Living Out God's Plan

Several years ago, the Singapore daily newspaper printed an entire section on the subject of love. One picture showed a young couple sitting beneath a tree looking into each other's eyes as ducks floated by on the pond in front of them. Many people have this concept of love: it is only for the young.

A second picture, however, will be permanently etched in my memory. It showed an elderly couple walking down a path. Instead of a beautiful pond, scraggly trees guided their way. But they walked together, holding hands! What a powerful picture of lasting commitment. Permanence is what God intended—two walking down the path of life together. Commitment provides a safe environment for love to grow and mature.

In the beginning, God created the man and the woman to be one flesh (Gen. 2:22-25). This oneness was described as cleaving, or being glued together, never to be the same if torn apart. In Matthew 19:6 Jesus described marriage with the word *joined. Joined* means *to yoke together, uniting in a permanent bond.* I believe that God's Holy Spirit is grieved over the state of many Christian marriages, originally designed as one wife and one husband for a lifetime.

Malachi 2:14 calls marriage a covenant relationship. The Bible pictures many covenant relationships. David and Jonathan had a covenant of friendship. They pledged that even after death their covenant would extend through their descendants (1 Sam. 20-42). God's covenant relationship with Israel is compared to a marriage relationship. The church is called the bride of Christ (Rev. 21:2). Covenant marriage for Christians is modeled after Christ's love for His church.

▛ Read Malachi 2:13-17 in your Bible. Why were the priests weeping?
☐ God sent a famine. ☐ God refused their sacrifices.
☐ God changed their rituals.

This passage was written to the priests. "This commandment is for you, O priests" (Mal. 2:1, NASB). The priests were presenting defiled foods on the altar by bringing lame and sick animal sacrifices. Then they cried out to the Lord and wondered why He did not accept their sacrifices. They expected God to accept left-overs—animals that they didn't want.

The priests were also divorcing their wives. They were treating what God had brought together in a holy covenant with disdain. God intended their marriages to produce godly offspring to bring light into a world living in darkness. God was weary (v. 17) of their uttered words, while they totally avoided their responsibilities to their marriages.

God desired to bless their marriages and their offspring. He urged them to guard their spirits (v. 15). In other words, they were to check out their hearts, to look at how they were dealing with their wives. Then, in very clear language God said, "I hate divorce" and called divorce "violence" (v. 16). Divorce does violence, or irreparable damage, to the divine plan for marriage, which was to be a committed relationship. Because the priests had lost their commitment to marriage, their relationship with God suffered.

▛ In regard to God's view of a marriage covenant, what is your level of commitment to your marriage? Place an X on the scale.

●━━━━━━━━━━━━━━━━━━━━━━━━━━●

a little commitment   some commitment   total commitment

Living in a Fallen World

God originally planned marriage as a permanent bond; however, fallen people living in a fallen world affected God's plan. In the Old Testament, Moses gave divorce as an option because of hard hearts—hearts that were turned away from God's goodness. In New Testament times, divorce was common. When the Pharisees asked Jesus about divorce in Matthew 19:1-12, they quoted the Old Testament to prove their point.

They hoped to discredit Jesus before the people by misusing the Word of God. They used a portion of the Word of God while adding their own interpretation. They said to Him, "Why then did Moses command that a man give his wife a certificate of divorce?" (v. 7).

The Pharisees were referring to the text of Deuteronomy 24:1-4. To understand the Pharisee's question and Jesus' answer, you must also understand this Deuteronomy passage.

Read Deuteronomy 24:1-4 and answer the following questions.

1. Who instigated the divorce and why?

_____

2. What did the wife do then? _____

_____

3. Why is the woman not to remarry her first husband?_____

_____

4. What interfered with God's original plan for marriage (v. 4)?

_____

The people of Israel had lost their distinctiveness by intermarriage, divorce, sinfulness, and rebellion against God. In the Hebrew language this passage is not a command for a man to divorce his wife if an indecency were found but was given as case law. Moses told a woman who found herself in this situation not to go back to her first husband. God didn't want them going back and forth because that would cheapen the marriage relationship and bring defilement.

Jesus was not tricked, and He responded that Moses did not command divorce but rather permitted divorce. He cut through to the real issue— a heart problem. " 'Because your hearts were hard' " (Matt. 19:8). God's people had allowed their hearts to become hardened to the will of God and no longer sought to obey Him. They were more focused on their own happiness than on God's intent for their marriages. They looked for a temporary "feel good" solution to their unhappiness rather than seeking God's permanent "be good" solution for their marriages.

God never intended that we divorce our partners, but because of our sinful natures and God's compassion, He provided a way out in specific circumstances. Without a certificate of divorce, a woman would be stoned to death; with this certificate, she was permitted to remarry. The women in that day were vulnerable members of society. Requiring a written letter of divorce made a husband think twice before throwing out his wife. Moses' provision protected women from neglect and abuse by their husbands.

Living Out of God's Goodness

God desires your good, and your marriages are very important to Him. Unhappiness and difficulties often arise out of our own sinful hearts rather than from circumstances and people. Our thoughts can totally sabotage our commitment level by focusing us on our husband's negative aspects instead of on God's sufficiency and grace extended to us just for this time.

The Lord is compassionate and gracious, slow to anger, abounding in love.
Psalm 103:8

Are any thoughts negatively affecting your commitment to your marriage? Take the time today to ask the Lord to bring to your mind anything that is keeping you from loving your husband. It may be thoughts of what it would have been like if you had married someone else. Or, it may be comparing your husband to other men. Confess these to the Lord and ask Him to replace these thoughts with pure and holy ones. God will forgive you and change your heart this very day!

It is so easy to get into the habit of blaming your lack of joy on your husband. Is this truth? The Scriptures plainly teach that joy is a fruit of the Spirit. Even though much of your subjective happiness depends on how your husband treats you, your joy can only come from God and trusting in His goodness!

Will you rest upon this fact of His goodness? How has God shown His goodness to you in a very real way? Thank Him for each way that He brings to mind. Write your prayer in the space provided.

Dear God, _____

_____

_____

Day 3

Lasting Commitment

A woman is bound to her husband as long as he lives. 1 Corinthians 7:39

I have a friend who plays the piano beautifully. I love to sit in a comfortable chair with my eyes closed listening to her play. Once I came to her home after she had just spent hours practicing. She was heavy with perspiration and looked totally spent.

Marriage may at times seem arduous and difficult, but just as commitment is necessary to playing beautiful piano music, we must remain faithful to to our partners, even when our efforts do not seem to produce any "music."

For this reason a man will leave his father and mother and be united to his wife, and they will become one flesh.
Genesis 2:24

In our weeks together, we have openly admitted our imperfections and willingly declared our need for divine assistance—God's Spirit. Scripture has affirmed every point we have studied. We have not built a case on psychology or culture. We have time and again returned to God's original design for marriage in Genesis 2.

Because we live in a fallen world, and sin is a reality, we must also look seriously at what God's Word says about the subject of divorce and the Christian. Divorce was a controversial issue in Jesus' day, just as it is now.

Jesus' Teaching on Divorce

Yesterday we referenced Jesus' encounter with the Pharisees over the question of divorce.

Read Matthew 19:1-12 in your Bible. Why do you think the Pharisees asked these questions?
- [ ] They wanted to trick Jesus.
- [ ] They trusted Jesus' teachings.
- [ ] They wanted more information.

The Pharisees were very jealous because great crowds were following Jesus. From all around, people flocked to hear His words and see the miracles He performed. His radical words brought conviction. Jesus called on the people to embrace His kingdom with their hearts and not just go through the motions by outwardly obeying rabbinical laws.

The Pharisees, wearing their special robes and tassels that designated them as religious leaders, addressed Jesus in front of the crowds. They were seeking to embarrass Jesus as they brought up the subject of divorce and remarriage, knowing full well what Jesus taught on this subject. Divorce was rampant, and the Pharisees were sure the people would not follow Jesus if they knew He was teaching something that would cramp their lifestyle (see Matt. 5:27-32).

The Pharisees asked Jesus if it were lawful to divorce for any cause at all. This was a trick question, and two rabbinical schools had given two different interpretations of Deuteronomy 24:1-4. One school said that the only acceptable reason for divorce was adultery. The other school said that anything displeasing to the husband was a valid reason for divorce.

The Pharisees laid a trap for Jesus, supposing his answer would make one school or the other angry. Instead, Jesus directed them to God's original plan for marriage. God created the marriage relationship; therefore, we should not separate what God joins.

Jesus then pointed out clearly that Moses only *permitted* divorce because of the hardness of their hearts. The Pharisees had mistaken God's gracious provision in permitting divorce in certain circumstances for His having ordained divorce. Jesus identified the real problem—their hearts.

Often, my heart has been "hard" to a message preached or a word of correction spoken. Later, I wish I had listened. How I grieve because of those times! Do you find yourself missing God's will for your life because your heart is not listening to what He has to say?

What About Adultery?

Read Matthew 19:9. This passage has caused much debate among scholars and theologians. Some say that divorce after adultery is permitted but not remarriage. Others say that divorce and remarriage are both permitted in the case of adultery.

I tell you that anyone who divorces his wife, except for marital unfaithfulness, and marries another woman commits adultery.
Matthew 19:9

Do you believe that adultery should always result in divorce? (circle)
☐ yes ☐ not sure ☐ no

Tell why: _____

_____

Mark 10:2-9 records the same incident but does not mention adultery. The intent of Jesus' teaching was to clearly break from Jewish legalism, while focusing on a far more important task: examining the heart. The

Mark passage holds both men and women accountable for the way they regard their marriages.

We may not be able to settle the issue of divorce and remarriage in the case of adultery for our day, but we must not miss Jesus' revolutionary teaching. He made it clear that throwing wives aside by divorce was not in God's original plan. He also stressed that women have a responsibility to their marriages.

What are some specific ways you can strengthen your commitment to your marriage?

1._____

2._____

3._____

Paul's Teachings on Divorce

Paul addressed the subject of divorce in I Corinthians 7. This passage was written to Gentile Christians who had come from a life of temple prostitution, polygamy, and multiple marriages. These new Christians had many questions about God's standard for marriage and sexuality.

Read I Corinthians 7:10-11. What was Paul's general view toward marital commitment?
- [ ] remain married to your present partner
- [ ] find a Christian partner
- [ ] remain unmarried

From whom did Paul receive this command? _____

Paul affirmed the teachings of Jesus. He urged permanence and reconciliation. In addition, Paul gave counsel regarding an unbelieving spouse who chose to terminate the marriage. In such cases, the principle of peace took precedence over the believing spouse staying in the marriage.

The bond of marriage can be broken by death (Rom. 7:2), adultery (Matt. 19:9), or an unbeliever's decision to leave the marriage. By implication, the permission for a widow to remarry (I Cor. 7:39-40) because the bond is broken, extends to the case where she is no longer "bound" (I Cor. 7:15). When an unbelieving spouse leaves, a Christian is free to marry another Christian.

In certain situations where sin has marred God's original intent, divorce may have to be considered because of the suffering of the wife and children, especially when their very lives are endangered. The principles of God's compassion and peace, as well as self-defense and the protection of the innocent, may override maintaining the marriage.

However, even in these hopeless situations, the consequences of divorce must not be overlooked. Divorce must not be initiated lightly but viewed as a last resort after every other recourse has failed.

Principles to Consider

When making a decision about divorce, consider these principles:

1. God's original design is a one flesh relationship for a lifetime. Sin and failure are realities in a fallen world. We must come to the Lord in humility, admitting our failures and acknowledging our gratitude for God's forgiveness.

2. Reconciliation is the goal. Before making a decision about separation, evaluate how this decision will affect the chances for reconciliation.

3. Don't give up easily. Even in the case of adultery, you are not required to seek a divorce. In the case of abuse, separation from an unpredictable and dangerous spouse can provide an opportunity for him to seek Christian counsel and demonstrate a changed lifestyle.

4. If the marriage ends, remember that God loves you despite your failures and sins. There is life after divorce.

5. If you consider remarriage, you are in greater need of premarital counseling than when you married the first time. You will need to work through the issues that led to divorce.

According to Malachi 2:14-16, God grieves over marriages that are not covenant relationships. However, while divorce falls short of God's plan, it is not unforgivable nor a greater sin than any other. All sin can be forgiven because of Christ's death on Calvary.

We must uphold God's standard for marriage while at the same time show compassion and sensitivity rather than dealing with people and situations legalistically. Each marriage situation has unique distinctions and must be approached with understanding and integrity.

Day 4

When Marriages Falter

Put your hope in God, for I will yet praise him, my Savior and my God.
Psalm 42:5-6

I first met Lillian in one of my marriage classes. I was impressed by the obvious peace and joy in her life, so when we had lunch together, I really did not expect the story that unfolded. Several years before when she was pregnant with her fourth child, she had found out that her husband of 20 years had been having a long-term affair and, in fact, had another household. Lillian was devastated! She attempted legal abortion more than five times but was unsuccessful. After her daughter was born, she went into severe depression and had to be hospitalized. She lost her job, had to be hospitalized again, and was angry at her husband and at God.

Eventually she gave an ultimatum to her husband: pick either her and the children or the other woman. He chose the other woman. One of her sons then went through a depression, and she was filled with self-blame and guilt. She struggled to get well but nothing seemed to help. A Christian support group encouraged her to forgive and let go for her own well-being, not because her husband deserved it. One day she gave up and prayed, "Lord, You know I can't handle this on my own. Just take over for me. I can't control anything."

Through these events she grew emotionally and spiritually. Yes, the pain continued, but she knew God was with her and enabled her to face each day with strength—sometimes just enough but always sufficient.

What do you do in a situation that seems beyond anything you can handle? Betrayed spouses tend to gravitate toward two extremes—*It's all my fault* or *It's all his fault*—neither of which is likely true. Rather than playing the blame game, concentrate on forgiveness and reconciliation with God's strength. God's Word contains principles that greatly help in painful situations. If you are in such a situation, focus on these principles before you make any permanent decision; they will help you as you seek God's will in your marriage, even if you are the only one seeking.

God can use you to save your marriage.

Betrayal is one of the greatest hurts that a woman can experience. When your trust in others is devastated, the inner core of who you are is affected.

Francis totally withdrew from friends when her husband had an emotional affair over the Internet. Both Francis and Lillian initially responded with anger, then wanted revenge, and finally felt despair.

After the initial shock, you may be filled with confusion. Depending on your personality style, you may strike out or withdraw. When you are faced with the decision to give up or save your marriage, realize that most marriages are saved by the initial efforts of one person.

In the face of betrayal, women often feel a devastating sense of low self-worth. As Christians we need to realize that God assures our significance and worth. God calls you by name, and you are His.

If your husband has left you or your world seems to crumble around you, God will be with you every step you take. Jesus said, " 'Whoever comes to me I will never drive away' " (John 6:37).

When Lillian put her trust in God and realized that God thought she was someone valuable, she was able to make it through each day. She realized that "with God, nothing shall be impossible" (Luke 1:37, KJV). She could get up in the morning; she could function as a mother. Even though the emotional pain was intense and sometimes almost overwhelming, she could depend on God. He was going to do a great work in her life; she didn't need to lose heart.

*Read 2 Corinthians 4:16-17 in the margin. Why does this Scripture

say we do not lose heart? _____

Gird your mind.

Peter said, "Therefore gird up the loins of your mind, be sober, and rest your hope fully upon the grace that is to be brought to you at the revelation of Jesus Christ" (1 Pet. 1:13, NKJV). Men in New Testament days wore tunics, and anytime they needed to run a race or get somewhere quickly, they would bunch their tunics in the center of their legs, bring the long garment up to their waist, and tuck the ends into their belt or sash. This freed their movement, and they were able to run unhindered. Peter applies this custom to one's thought processes. This passage encourages us to pull all of our thoughts together and put them under God's protection and wisdom.

Be careful from whom you get advice. Everyone gave Lillian advice—family members, work associates, and friends. She talked to pastors, Christian lay leaders, and her mother. She found later that some of the

*" 'Fear not, for I have
redeemed you;
I have summoned you
by name; you are mine.
When you pass through
the waters,
I will be with you;
and when you pass through
the rivers,
they will not sweep
over you.
When you walk through
the fire,
you will not be burned;
the flames will not set
you ablaze' "*
Isaiah 43:1-2

Therefore we do not lose heart. Even though our outward man is perishing, yet the inward man is being renewed day by day. For our light affliction, which is but for a moment, is working for us a far more exceeding and eternal weight of glory
2 Corinthians 4:16-17, NKJV

173

advice was biblical but much was meant only to give justification for her anger. Lillian became more confused than ever.

If possible, have a retreat with God. Get away from distractions and advice-givers, armed only with the Word of God. Women to whom I have given this advice say they gained God's strength during their private retreat. They were able to think back to this retreat and renew their awareness of God's strength to carry them through the days that followed. During this retreat, have tunnel vision—listen to no one other than the Lord. Oh ladies, God is trustworthy. He keeps His word, and He will not fail you as others have.

Fly by instruments.

What are we do do when we feel there is nothing we can do? Trust. Let me illustrate it this way. When I was growing up, my father had a private plane. I remember one particular trip when the weather was so bad that I couldn't see one foot in front of us. Having a captive audience, my Dad shared how pilots in weather like this cannot discern which direction they are flying or even whether they are right side up. Dad then turned the plane so that we were flying upside down. I was amazed at how disoriented I was even in that short time. He then explained that we were OK because we were flying by instruments—we would never go the wrong way. I could tell by his voice and the twinkle in his eyes that we would be all right, so I settled down and slept the rest of the trip.

Sometimes you cannot see the direction you need to go. God is your guiding instrument. Even when you feel as if you are losing your mind, God will direct you. When you don't know what to do, trust God. When you can't see beyond the pain and despair, trust God. When you don't see a way out, remember, "with God nothing will be impossible" (Luke 1:37, NKJV).

Put your faith in action.

Read Colossians 3:12-17 on the next page and underline what you are to do.

Oh ladies, you are chosen! God can use you in such a way that you will look back at your present circumstances and be amazed. After you have girded up the loins of your mind and prepared yourself to fly by instruments, you are ready to put your faith into action.

You can be kind, meek, and patient because your worth is from the Lord. You can actually be kind without being manipulative because all that you are doing is for the Lord. You can make it through each day because you have God's strength preparing you every step of the way.

Your husband or your circumstances may not change, but you know that you have a sufficiency of grace. " 'My grace is sufficient for you, for My strength is made perfect in weakness.' Therefore most gladly I will rather boast in my infirmities, that the power of Christ may rest upon me. Therefore I take pleasure in infirmities, in reproaches, in needs, in persecutions, in distresses, for Christ's sake. For when I am weak, then I am strong" (2 Cor. 12:9-10, NKJV).

You can forgive, because you know how much God has forgiven you and how you are His precious child. You know you have forgiven your husband when you are able to pray for your husband's good. You are able to live day by day because God's strength is available to you at the moment you need it.

You may wonder what happened to Lillian. She is still married but not reunited with her husband. However, she is filled with peace and hope. Does she have a reason for divorce with the freedom of remarriage? Yes, but she does not feel this is what God would have her do. Her final words to me the day we had lunch were words of empathy for those who are going through the shock of an adulterous husband—the hurt, rejection, emotional confusion, bitterness, and despair. Yet she still encourages ladies not to give up but to depend on the Lord. A committed heart has a different way of looking at the future.

 According to 2 Corinthians 5:7, how are we to walk? _____

We are to walk by faith and not by sight. When my family landed in the Philippines, we discovered that much of our earthly possessions had been stolen while still on the ship. Initially, we were shocked; then we were angry. I shed many tears over my sentimental things that were gone. Why would God allow this to happen when we were doing His work? God understood these feelings, but we did not remain in the depths of our negative emotions; instead, we entered God's freedom by walking in faith. Somehow we knew God would provide for us—and He did. Walking by faith is trusting in God's goodness and faithfulness to take care of us.

Is your marriage faltering? Do you need to walk by faith? Ask God to give you His encouragement. Write your prayer in the space on page 176.

Therefore, as God's chosen people, holy and dearly loved, clothe yourselves with compassion, kindness, humility, gentleness and patience. Bear with each other and forgive whatever grievances you may have against one another. Forgive as the Lord forgave you. And over all these virtues put on love, which binds them all together in perfect unity.

Let the peace of Christ rule in your hearts, since as members of one body you were called to peace. And be thankful. Let the word of Christ dwell in you richly as you teach and admonish one another with all wisdom, and as you sing psalms, hymns and spiritual songs with gratitude in your hearts to God. And whatever you do, whether in word or deed, do it all in the name of the Lord Jesus, giving thanks to God the Father through him.
Colossians 3:12-17

We walk by faith, not by sight.
2 Corinthians 5:7,
NASB

When Marriages Falter:
1. Gird your mind.
2. Fly by instruments.
3. Put your faith in action.

Dear God, _____

_____

_____

Day 5

A Committed Heart

I desire to do your will, O my God; your law is within my heart. Psalm 40:8

This study has been built on hope: hope for change and for God to work in your marriage. We have openly admitted our imperfections and have asked God to give us His divine assistance. Each point has been affirmed by Scripture. We know God can solve every marital problem.

Never underestimate the power of a woman who has yielded her life to God. If you have been trying the conventional methods to change your husband and marriage and nothing has seemed to work, perhaps you need to re-evaluate your motives. When you demand that your husband change, in effect you are saying that you cannot experience joy unless God somehow uses your husband to bring you joy. Ladies, joy is a fruit of the Spirit within you. God is ready to meet your needs, right now, apart from your husband, if you will only let Him. My prayer is that you would discover that joy in marriage is experiencing God and His faithfulness despite our unfaithfulness.

So what now?

When all our dreams for a perfect marriage and all our hopes for an intimate relationship are not met, despair and depression often set in. We ask, *Is this all there is to marriage? Will we never be happy?*

Some wives try to fill their emotional cups with motherhood; others seek fulfillment through work. Still others may substitute addictive behaviors, such as overspending or eating disorders. Many women believe that if they could just move to a new location, they would be happy again. Others try to quench their thirst through climbing the social ladder.

If you have found yourself putting your hope in any of these sources, I have good news for you. At this point in your life, you can come to God and truly say, *I need You. I can't live alone anymore. I have nothing apart from You.*

So what are we to do? We need to refocus our expectations and place our hearts on a totally different source.

A Heart That Abides in God's Word

 Read Luke 10:38-42 in your Bible. Describe Mary and Martha.

_____

_____

_____

> *"The Lord answered and said to her, "Martha, Martha, you are worried and bothered about so many things; but only a few things are necessary, really only one, for Mary has chosen the good part, which shall not be taken away from her."*
> Luke 10:41-42, NASB

Recently a Bible study leader asked us to choose one Bible character we most resembled and a second one we would most like to resemble. Several women responded that they were most like Martha, busy doing needed activities but, for the most part, reacting to the circumstances in life rather than acting on them. Often, our daily pressures to keep a home running smoothly consume us. We are reacting, rather than choosing the most important action of all.

What did Mary do that earned the praise of our Lord? She enjoyed His presence. She made a choice that went against the culture of the day. Women were not allowed to be students. Mary studied at the feet of Jesus. Commit yourself to daily study of God's Word. Our heart for the Lord should be like a boiling pot, excited and passionate about God.

 How would you rate your heart condition?

●———————————————————————————●

passionless about God   passionate about God

Only through daily time spent in God's Word can you and I have God's perspective so that we can walk by faith. I know firsthand how difficult it is to develop the habit of drawing near to God. I have used many excuses, such as "I'll just spend more time tomorrow."

I have the most consistency in my personal Bible study when I spend time with the Lord at the same time and the same place every day. The place is very important to me, because it is our place, the Lord's and mine, and I know He waits there for me every day.

A Heart That Prays

Through prayer, our relationship with the Lord deepens. As you spend regular, daily, unhurried time in prayer, an intimate relationship develops. Prayer increases our faith. As we see God answer our prayers and work in our lives, our faith grows.

 Read Luke 11:5-13 in your Bible. How do these verses encourage us to discover God's best for us?

_____

_____

The answer is persistent prayer. We are to continually seek and knock until we find God's answer. In Him we find the joy and peace that are not affected by people or circumstances. Oh, ladies, God is faithful and He has promised to give you His Spirit if you just ask. This is what you are seeking. This is the life God has promised. You can be filled to overflowing.

Prayer will also improve your relationship with your husband. When you are praying for your husband's good, you are more likely to think of him positively. You also find yourself more motivated to care for him. God changes our hearts as we pray. Oh ladies, when your relationship with the Lord has the reigning position in your heart, your thoughts, words, actions, and commitment to your husband will reflect the heart of God.

Now let me ask you. Do you think praying—even for just five minutes a day—could change your marriage? Will you try it for one week? Will you take your concerns about your husband to the Lord?

 In the margin, list some of what you learned and ways God answered your prayers.

A Heart That Obeys

Obedience is not a popular word. Many women really don't like the idea of being submissive to their husbands, but as we learned in week 3, rebellion against our husbands is really rebellion against God. Throughout this study, we have established principles from the Word of God, and now comes the crisis—will you do what it says? Will you give your desires to the Lord and seek to do His will?

Although David sinned greatly, he was praised as a person who sought to know God's heart and do His will.

 Read Proverbs 4:23-27 in your Bible. List ways from this passage to guard your heart.

_____

_____

"After He had removed him, He raised up David to be their king, concerning whom He also testified and said, 'I have found David the son of Jesse, a man after My heart, who will do all My will.'"
Acts 13:22, NASB

If you have hurt your husband by your words and actions—no matter what he has done—call sin just that, sin. Oh, but when we confess, God will forgive us! If you have a need to apologize, don't delay. Satan loves for us to fail to obey God in our marriages.

If you have been holding on to a pattern of disobedience, take these steps today:

1. Give God your hurts. Time, as we have learned, doesn't heal hurts, bitterness, or anger. Only God can heal through His unconditional love and abiding presence. He is your comforter (2 Cor. 1:3-4).

2. Choose forgiveness. Forgiveness is a choice, not a feeling. The question is not *do you feel like forgiving*, but *will you*? Will you release the hurt or will you be held captive by it for the rest of your life?

3. Confess your sins. Quit confessing your husband's faults and confess your own! Take responsibility for your own actions in your marriage. God stands ready to forgive you (1 John 1:9).

 Can you pinpoint any behavior in your life that calls for a heart response of confession?

_____

_____

179

Where can you find lasting fulfillment and joy? Knowing that you have looked for joy in all the wrong places may be the first step for you. Then discover God's best for you. Is God's desire your desire? Does your heart follow after God? Are you committed to God first and then to your husband and your marriage? Obedience is a foundational stepping-stone for having a heart committed to God and to your husband.

If this has not been your experience, will you pray the following prayer along with me or write your own in the margin?

Dear Lord, I want to experience You to the fullest. I release people, things, and circumstances from making me happy. I want You to fill my life. Help me to love my husband and others with Your *agape* love. I can do this because You have filled my emotional cup to overflowing with Your Spirit. Give me Your wisdom to be the best possible wife and mother. Help me through my difficulties to guide others into the truth that I have learned from You. Amen.

God is in the business of miracles, and my prayer for each of you is that He will work miracles in your life and in your marriage. I pray that you have found joy being the woman that God redeemed you to be and that you will make a positive difference in your marriage. May God shower His lavish love on you.

Leader Guide

This Leader Guide will help you facilitate an introductory session and eight group sessions for the study of *Women Making a Difference in Marriage: Building Love, Joy, and Commitment.* Group sessions are designed for one hour in length. If you have more than one hour, extend the time allotted for discussion.

Supplies

Have on hand an attendance sheet, extra Bibles, pens or pencils, and member books. For the first couple of sessions, supply name tags.

Arrange the chairs in a semicircle with the opening nearest the door. Sit as a part of the group. If you do not have a markerboard and markers, bring tear sheets, markers, and masking tape as called for in the teaching plans.

Distribute the books during the introductory session or at least one week in advance of session I. Use an attendance sheet that allows room for phone numbers, email addresses, and home addresses as a means of contacting absentees during the week.

Publicity

Begin your publicity at least six weeks in advance of the introductory session. Since this subject will appeal to persons who do not attend your church, place fliers or posters in businesses and offices near your church. Leave advertisements in doctors' and dentists' offices, as well as childcare providers and schools in your area.

Make use of free advertising in newspapers and on television and radio stations. Promote the study in worship bulletins, church newsletters, and on hallway bulletin boards. Send written invitations to women who serve in leadership capacities in your church.

Prayer Support

Bathe the study in prayer! Enlist prayer partners who will pray from the time the study is announced until it concludes. As persons sign up for the study, encourage them to begin praying for themselves, other group members, and the group leader. Consider gathering in the room where you will be meeting for a time of prayer prior to the introductory session.

Some groups may want to assign prayer partners during the length of the study, or prayer partners can rotate during the study.

Group Membership

This study is designed for married women and is not premarital education. Since many of the learning activities are based on marital experiences, a single woman would find it difficult to participate in the discussion.

Some of the group members may be married to non-Christians or to men who do not attend your church. This study will address issues related to their situations, as well as women whose husbands are active church members. Seek to encourage each participant by your prayers and after-session phone calls.

Confidentiality will be essential as members share questions and issues in their marriages. An opportunity to sign a confidentiality agreement is offered in the introductory session. If you do not wish to have members sign a statement, state the need for keeping confidences in the session.

An intergenerational group works well with this topic, since wives with more experience can help guide younger wives. Avoid giving advice; rather, say something similar to "When in this situation, I have found it helpful to ..."

Group Leadership

This study does not require a leader with a perfect marriage! As you deal with questions and issues, demonstrate your own willingness to learn and grow in your marriage relationship.

The teaching plans follow a discussion format. Seek to involve all of the members in the discussion. Re-direct questions addressed to you. "What would you say to this question?" Do not center the discussion around yourself and your marriage issues.

This resource is a guide to discussion. It should not be used to restrict discussion only to the suggested questions or activities. Adapt the teaching plans to your group. Be flexible, prepared to pick up on members' interests.

Some of the activities are more personal in nature. You may wish to divide your group into subgroups of twos or threes (triads) for these activities to allow more people to share in a more comfortable subgroup environment.

Encourage group members to build listening skills by listening carefully to each other. Members can powerfully bless each other as concerns are taken seriously.

Group members will be tempted to mention ways they would like for their husbands to change. Firmly remind them that this study focuses on the wife's role in marriage enrichment.

After each session, evaluate the group experience. Did everyone participate? Does someone need encouragement? Is someone not completing the assignments? Use notes, phone calls, or email to follow up on your observations.

Childcare

Childcare may significantly affect attendance. If possible, provide childcare at the church. Consider enlisting senior adults or older teenagers to help with childcare, or help participants arrange homes where children from two or more families might combine resources to meet childcare needs.

Introductory Session

Before the Session

1. Prepare an attendance sheet for use each week. Provide name tags and markers.
2. Have copies of *Women Making a Difference in Marriage* available to distribute. If payment is expected, prepare a cash box to make change.
3. Bring a calculator to add the number of years of marriage represented by the group.
4. Mount a tear sheet on a focal wall and label it "Issues." Place a marker on the floor beneath it.
5. Duplicate copies of a statement of confidentiality that members will sign during the session, or write on a markerboard or another tear sheet a statement which members will affirm orally.

During the Session

1. Upon arrival, direct participants to sign the attendance sheet, giving their names and contact information, and make name tags. Give each one a copy of the member book.
2. Ask them to go directly to the "Issues" tear sheet and list one or more topics they would like to discuss during this study.
3. Begin the session by introducing yourself and telling about your immediate family. If possible, share a humorous story from your marriage to break the ice with any visitors. Then encourage participants to introduce themselves in a similar fashion.

4. As participants share, use the calculator to total the years of marriage experience represented by the group. After the last person has shared, announce the total. Say, *We have many years of marriage represented in this room. I am looking forward to learning from you as well as from our workbook.*

5. Read selected statements or questions from the tear sheet. Explain that you will keep these issues in mind throughout the study.

6. Invite participants to turn to the Table of Contents on page 3. Read aloud the eight titles and point out that these represent eight aspects women need to cultivate to make a difference in their marriages.

7. Select a good reader to read "About the Author" and "About the Study" on page 4. Summarize the key information in the "Introduction" on pages 5-7, or ask a volunteer to read it to the group. If you do not read it in the session, assign the "Introduction" as part of the reading assignment for week 1.

8. Point out that the nature of this study requires confidentiality. Say, *We need to agree not to tell someone else's story.* Have members sign a commitment card or affirm orally a statement of confidentiality.

9. Say, *Although your husbands will be aware of your workbook study, this course is written to wives, not couples. Several times the author will ask you to share something with your husband, seek his forgiveness, or ask him questions. Unless specifically asked to talk to your husband, avoid sharing insights you have learned. Your words may be interpreted as an attempt to change him, in which case he may react negatively. Let your words and actions over the next weeks speak for themselves. Do not use the words of this workbook as "ammunition" pointed at him. This course is about what you can do to improve your marriage, not what he can do.*

10. Ask participants to turn to week 1 and scan the five lessons. Point out the importance of completing the learning activities. Ask them to read the week's content and complete the learning activities prior to group session 1.

11. If individuals are paying for their workbooks, collect the money or announce how you want to receive payment. Discuss any housekeeping issues, such as childcare, meeting times, and place (if it is different from this session).

12. Close the session with prayer. If your group is made up of persons who do not know each other well, use discretion in calling for prayer requests. List requests on your personal paper and pray for them during the coming week.

After the Session

1. Read the content and complete the learning activities for week 1.

2. Review the lesson plan for week 1. Collect suggested materials and supplies.

3. Make it a point to contact each participant and welcome her to the group. Be available to answer questions or address any concerns.

4. Pray faithfully for yourself, group members, and the prayer requests mentioned in the introductory session. Ask follow-up questions as appropriate at the next session.

Week 1: Lasting Joy

1. As participants enter, have them sign the attendance sheet and attach a name tag to their clothing. Have on hand extra copies of the member book. If members are paying for their books, collect money from those who did not pay at the introductory session.

2. Open with prayer. Thank God for the spiritual fruit of joy that is available only through Him.

3. Spend 2-3 minutes reviewing key concepts from the introductory session. Ask volunteers to:
   - name several of the eight aspects women need to cultivate to make a difference in their marriages;
   - explain what life experiences prepared the author to write this study;
   - tell why confidentiality is important to the group's discussion.

   Allow opportunity for questions or comments before you discuss week I.

4. Use the following questions/statements as discussion starters for a review of week I. The bullets in parentheses represent statements or actions for the leader.

Day 1
- How should believing we are uniquely made in the image of God impact the way we view ourselves? What did you learn from Katie's story on page 10?
- Why is it a burden for your husband to be the source of your self-esteem (p. 11)?
- What or who has helped you to be thankful for how God made you?

Day 2
- Before this study, how did you feel about being your husband's "helper"? Has your opinion changed? If so, in what ways?

- In what ways do you function as your husband's helper?
- How do your words serve as a protection for your husband's heart?
- How are you a recreational companion for your husband?

Day 3
- In your own words, tell what you think it means to be a "suitable helper" (Gen. 2:20).
- How are we to be "godly counterparts" to our husbands? What detracts from our complementary function?
- (Without calling for answers, discuss the implications of the learning activities on page 18. Are we putting God first?)
- What can we do to show our husbands that they are our most important earthly relationships (p. 19)?
- Why might Satan want to oppose you during this study (p. 20)? (Pause to pray for God's protection and for perseverance.)

Day 4
- Explain how Satan deceived Eve. How does Satan use these same tactics today?
- What effects did sin have on the first marriage? List ways our sin natures impact marriage today.
- (Explain God's plan for restoring mankind on page 25. Invite anyone who may have asked Jesus into her heart to express her decision to the group or to remain after the session to talk with you. Follow up with persons who make decisions or express interest in accepting Christ.

Day 5
- Why can't joy be based on people, circumstances, or possessions?
- What is joy based on? Read Galatians 5:22-23.

• How is joy possible in the midst of conflict (p. 27)? How is joy in marriage restored (p. 28)?
• (Allow volunteers to share their answers to the learning activity on page 28.)

5. Assign week 2 to be completed during the coming week.
6. Ask for prayer requests and pray for individuals and for this study.

Week 2: Unfailing Love

1. Place the attendance sheet and name tags (optional) by the door. Greet members as they arrive and have them sign the sheet.
2. Open with prayer. Thank God for His unfailing love and for the opportunity to share His love with others.
3. Refer to the learning goals in the margin on page 8 to recall key concepts from week 1.
4. Use the following questions/statements as discussion starters for a review of week 2.

Day 1
• Share beliefs about love you learned from your family.
• How do these affect your views toward love: 1) past experiences; 2) culture; 3) God's Word.
• Explain the difference between loving your husband in your own strength and allowing God to love him through you (p. 35).

Day 2
• Explain the difference between love as a choice and love as an emotional response.
• Share your response to the learning activity near the bottom of page 36.
• How do thoughts impact words and behavior (p. 37)?

• (Repeat together Psalm 19:14 from the margin of page 38.)

Day 3
• What is a practical way you can show affection to your husband (p. 39)?
• What are some ways you can encourage your husband (p. 40)?
• Is your husband your best friend? If so, tell why.
• From pages 41-42, name some ways to develop friendship love.
• (Encourage members who did not complete the activity at the bottom of page 42 to do so this week.)

Day 4
• Explain the difference between romantic and sexual love.
• What words or behaviors tend to squelch romantic love?
• What are some practical ways to build a climate for romance?

Day 5
• Explain ways God's love (*agape*) distinctly differs from human love. How is God's love like human love?
• (Without calling for responses, discuss the implications of the learning activity on page 49.)
• (Ask a volunteer to read 1 Corinthians 13:4-7. Review each of the qualities of *agape* love.)
• Share your responses to the learning activity at the bottom of page 50.

5. Assign week 3 to be completed during the coming week.
6. Ask for prayer requests and pray for individuals and for this study.

Week 3: Willing Submission

1. Place the attendance sheet by the door. Greet members as they arrive and have them sign the sheet.
2. Open with prayer. Thank God for His authority in our lives. Thank Him for earthly authorities. Pray for your national and church leaders.
3. Refer to the learning goals on page 30 to recall key concepts of week 2. Say, *Love, joy, and peace are the first three fruits of the Spirit (Gal. 5:22-23). Today we will discuss how the biblical principle of submission brings us peace.* Read I Corinthians 14:33. Explain that submission to authority is God's plan for bringing peace—not disorder—to our lives.
4. Use the following questions/statements as discussion starters for a review of week 3.

Day 1

- Why does God want submission to authority to be willing and voluntary?
- Read Romans 13:1-2. Why is rebelling against authority rebelling against God?
- How does a rebellious spirit open us to Satan's attacks (p. 55)?
- How is submitting to God a way to resist Satan? (Read James 4:7.)
- Recall the three choices we can make in regard to submission (p. 56).

Day 2

- (Without calling for specific responses, review the pitfalls of each battleground listed on page 58.)
- Using the outline on pages 59-60, list practical ways you can develop the qualities of a peace-maker in your home.

Day 3

- (Ask members to share responses to the learning activity at the bottom of page 61.)
- What are two criteria that enable believers to submit to each other (Eph. 5:21)?
- What does it mean to submit to your husband "as to the Lord" (Eph 5:22)?
- Explain why submission does not indicate inequality or inferiority.

Day 4

- Why might it be said that husbands have the harder role in marriage (p. 65)?
- How was Sarah a model of submission (p. 67)?
- What advice does Peter give the wife of an unbeliever (p. 68)?

Day 5

- (Review each of the guidelines for submission on page 70.)
- What counsel does the author give women in abusive situations (p. 71)?
- How can caring about yourself and being submissive to your husband work together in your life?
- (As a group, say Philippians 4:19 together.)

5. Assign week 4 to be completed during the coming week.
6. Use the remainder of the time for prayer requests and prayer for individuals and for this study.

Week 4: Virtuous Character

1. Place the attendance sheet by the door. Greet members as they arrive and have them sign the sheet.
2. Open with prayer. Thank God for His virtuous character and His righteousness. Thank Him that through Jesus Christ we can "put on the new self, created to be like God in true righteousness and holiness" (Eph 4:24).
3. Refer to the learning goals on page 52 to recall key concepts in week 3. Introduce this week's topic by asking, *Have any of you had a "character building experience" such as the one Lana described on page 73?* Be prepared to share a personal experience if you have one.
4. Use the following questions/statements as discussion starters for a review of week 4.

Day 1
- How do you feel about being a role model of a godly wife? (Note the author's point that we should begin where we are, making one change at a time.)
- What is your definition of character? Why does our culture place little value on character?
- What are some ways that we can build trust in a relationship?

Day 2
- In what ways is it helpful to view Proverbs 31:10-31 as stages in a woman's life?
- (Divide into two small groups. Ask one group to discuss ways to deal with the problem of comparison and the other to deal with the problem of perfectionism. Provide tear sheets and markers for each group. After 3-5 minutes of discussion, call for group reports.)
- React to the comparison between rearing children and running a household and holding a wet bar of soap (p. 81).
- How do you balance activities outside the home and caring for needs at home?

Day 3
- (Divide into two groups. Assign one group the mid-life years (pp. 83-84), and the other the later years (pp. 84-85). Ask groups to report on the character traits that were prominent in each stage. provide tear sheets and markers. After 3-5 minutes, call for reports.)
- (Allow volunteers to share their responses to the learning activity at the top of page 86.)

Day 4
- How can those who work at home avoid the dangers of idleness, gossip, and slander?
- Can you do anything to make the atmosphere in your home more godly?
- Why is grumbling not allowed (p. 87)?
- (Discuss the issue of working outside the home if this is a concern for your group.)

Day 5
- Tell about some ways you minister to others through your church and community.
- How have you been able to use your home as an avenue of service (neighbors, friends, needy persons)?
- (Say together Proverbs 3:5-6. Ask volunteers to share what these verses mean to them.)
- What was your response to the last learning activity on page 93?

5. Assign week 5 to be completed during the coming week.
6. Use the remainder of the time for prayer requests and prayer for individuals and for this study.

Week 5: Godly Communication

1. Place the attendance sheet by the door. Greet members as they arrive and have them sign the sheet.
2. Open with prayer. Thank God for desiring to have a personal relationship with us. Thank Him for prayer, our means of communication with Him. Pray for a heart to honor Him in all we say.
3. Refer to the learning goals in the margin on page 73 to recall key concepts from week 4. Introduce this week's topic by asking members to react to the author's statement on page 94 that "The quantity of words does not necessarily improve communication. ... What we need is quality of communication."
4. Use the following questions/statements as discussion starters for a review of week 5.

Day 1
• What does accepting reality have to do with improved communication?
• (Allow volunteers to share their responses to the learning activity in the middle of page 96.)
• What does body language have to do with improved communication? (Ask volunteers to demonstrate helpful and unhelpful body language when sending clear communication.)
• What are some of your ideas for clearer communication?

Day 2
• How do we treat others like dolls who have to fit in to our worlds? (see p. 100)
• What does the author mean by "reflective listening"?
• (Review the three ways to improve listening skills at the bottom of page 102.)

• What did you learn about your husband this past week by just listening (p. 103).

Day 3
• Summarize the problems we will face if we fill our minds with negative thoughts.
• How do we discipline our minds?
• (Assign the Scriptures in the learning activity at the top of page 106 to be read aloud. Then read 2 Corinthians 10:5.)

Day 4
• React to the statement (p. 107): "Our words in the home set the atmosphere of the whole house."
• (Assign each of the hurtful words on pages 107-109—gossip, lying, criticism, and folly—to four individuals, pairs, or triads. Ask them to explain why and how they are hurtful and to list ways we can avoid them. Call for reports.)
• (Review the source of hurtful words from pages 109-110.)

Day 5
• What is the advantage in communication that we have over unbelievers (top of page 111)?
• (Assign each of the characteristics of healing works to an individual, pair, or triad. Ask them to illustrate the characteristics and list ways we can cultivate them. Call for reports.)
• (Ask a volunteer to read Proverbs 15:4 from her Bible or from page 108.) How are healing words like a tree of life (p. 114)?

5. Assign week 6 to be completed during the coming week.
6. Use the remainder of the time for prayer requests and prayer for individuals and for this study.

Week 6: Christ-Centered Emotions

1. Place the attendance sheet by the door. Greet members as they arrive and have them sign the sheet.
2. Open with prayer. Thank God for making us with emotions such as love and joy. Ask Him to help us to express our emotions in a Christ-honoring way.
3. Refer to the learning goals in the margin on page 94 to recall key concepts from week 5. Introduce this week's topic by recalling a personal incident when you wished you could put spoken words back into your mouth. Say, *Today we are looking at the power of the tongue to build or destroy relationships.*
4 Use the following questions/statements as discussion starters for a review of week 6.

Day 1
- (Read Proverbs 18:21 on page 117. Ask, *What are some positive "fruit" of the tongue? negative fruit?*)
- React to this statement: We produce sweet words by planting godly fruit.
- Summarize how the tongue is like 1) a horse's bit; 2) a rudder; 3) a fire; 4) a fountain (pp. 117-119).
- What was your response to the learning activity at the bottom of page 119?

Day 2
- Name and illustrate five unhelpful ways to deal with conflict (pp. 120-121).
- Summarize each of the five principles from God's Word about handling conflict (pp. 122-123).
- (If appropriate, ask someone in the group to share a recurring conflict from her marriage. Lead the group to apply the five principles to her situation, but don't give advice. Watch the time. Close the discussion with prayer for her and her marriage.)

Day 3
- React to this statement (p. 125): "The one who makes you angry is yourself—your feelings, your thoughts, your own imaginations."
- Describe the difference between righteous and unrighteous anger (p. 126). What are we to do with unrighteous anger (p. 127)?
- (Review the key points about what to do with anger from the material on page 128.)

Day 4
- React to this statement (p. 129): "Worry is an outgrowth of fear."
- Why does worry dishonor God (p. 129)?
- What three good gifts has God given us to replace fear (p. 130)?
- (Allow volunteers to share their responses to the learning activity on page 131.)
- (Read together Philippians 4:6 on page 132.)

Day 5
- What are some false beliefs about forgiveness we need to put away?
- (Review each of the five aspects of God's standard for forgiveness on pages 134-136.)
- (If someone in the group is wrestling with the issue of forgiveness, allow time for questions and comments from the group.)

5. Assign week 7 to be completed during the coming week.
6. Use the remainder of the time for prayer requests and prayer for individuals and for this study.

Week 7: Sexual Fulfillment

1. Place the attendance sheet by the door. Greet members as they arrive and have them sign the sheet.
2. Open with prayer. Thank God for making us male and female. Thank Him for the good gift of sexuality. Ask Him to help us honor Him in expressing this good gift.
3. Refer to the learning goals in the margin on page 115 to recall key concepts from week 6. Introduce this session by referring to the author's statement on page 137 that "you may have mixed feelings about our studying this topic." Allow opportunity for members to express their feelings.
4. Use the following questions/statements as discussion starters for a review of week 7.

Day 1

- (Review each of the misconceptions about sexuality from pages 138-140. Emphasize the negative consequences of holding these opinions.)
- (Allow opportunity for members to share sexual attitudes from their families of origin. Discuss how these attitudes influence us today as wives and mothers. Point out that childhood experiences do not have to determine our adult feelings and actions.)
- In your own words, explain God's plan for marriage.

Day 2

- (Allow volunteers to share their responses to the learning activities on pages 143-144.)
- Explain why sexual infidelity is a violation of God's plan for marriage.

Day 3

- What was your response to the learning activity at the top of page 146?
- Explain the biblical reason for interrupting intimacy in marriage. Why is this to be a temporary action?
- (Discuss the author's opinion that husbands and wives should discuss openly their sexual preferences.)
- How does a healthy sex life promote fidelity in marriage?
- How do men and women differ in sexual arousal? What actions help us to respond positively to these differences?

Day 4

- How did you respond to the first learning activity on page 150?
- How did you respond to the learning activity on page 152?
- How does making excuses dishonor God and undermine intimacy in marriage?

Day 5

- (Ask two volunteers to review Cathy's story and Valerie's story from page 154.)
- (Assign each of the typical reactions on page 155 to volunteers. Ask them to explain why these are not helpful in the situation.)
- (Review Hosea's story and what it teaches us about God's love for us and how we are to respond to others.)

5. Assign week 8 to be completed during the coming week.
6. Use the remainder of the time for prayer requests and prayer for individuals and for this study.

Week 8: Covenant Commitment

1. If possible, as you greet each person, give her a personalized thank-you note for participating in this study.
2. Open with prayer. Thank God for His covenant faithfulness to us. Ask for His blessings as we seek to be faithful covenant partners in our marriages.
3. Refer to the learning goals in the margin on page 137 to recall key concepts from week 7. Introduce this session by referring to the author's statement on page 159 that "Quitting the marriage is an all too quick first response for those experiencing difficulties." Allow opportunity for members to express their feelings.
4. Use the following questions/statements as discussion starters for a review of week 8.

Day 1

- What is the basis for Christian hope (pp. 160-161)?
- React to this statement (p. 161): "Your responsibility is to respond to life's events in the way that pleases God."
- Explain how Christians are priests, similar to the role of the High Priest in the Old Testament.
- Why is there no need to despair (p. 163)?

Day 2

- What interfered with God's original plan for marriage (p. 166)?
- Illustrate how negative thoughts can affect your level of commitment to your marriage.
- Why do we find it easy to blame our lack of joy on our husbands? What is our real source of joy?

Day 3

- Summarize Jesus' teachings on divorce from Matthew 19:1-12.
- Summarize Paul's teachings on divorce from I Corinthians 7.
- (Review the principles on page 171. Invite questions and discussion.)

Day 4

- (Review each of the principles for help in painful situations on pages 172-175. Invite questions and discussion, based on the needs of your group.)
- What are some ways you can befriend someone going through a painful time in her marriage? (Remind members that giving advice or playing counselor are not recommended actions!)

Day 5

- React to this statement (p. 176): "Joy in marriage is experiencing God and His faithfulness despite our unfaithfulness."
- (Encourage members to take the author's advice on page 178 to pray for their husbands and marriages every day and especially to pray for their husband's good.)
- (Discuss the importance of confession to God and to our husbands when we wound with our words or deeds.)
- (Say aloud together the prayer on page 180.)

5. As time permits, turn to the Table of Contents on page 3 and review the eight topics covered in this study.
6. Use the remainder of the time for prayer requests and prayer for individuals and for continued implementation of the principles contained in this study.

102613

CHRISTIAN GROWTH STUDY PLAN

Preparing Christians to Serve

In the **Christian Growth Study Plan (formerly Church Study Course)**, this book *Women Making a Difference in Marriage* is a resource for course credit in the subject area Home/Family of the Christian Growth category of diploma plans. To receive credit, read the book, complete the learning activities, show your work to your pastor, a staff member or church leader, then complete the following information. This page may be duplicated. Send the completed page to:

Christian Growth Study Plan
• One LifeWay Plaza • Nashville, TN 37234-0117
• FAX: (615)251-5067 • Email: cgspnet@lifeway.com
For information about the Christian Growth Study Plan, refer to the current Christian Growth Study Plan Catalog. Your church office may have a copy. If not, request a free copy from the Christian Growth Study Plan office (615/251-2525). Also available online at www.lifeway.com/cgsp/catalog.

WOMEN MAKING A DIFFERENCE IN MARRIAGE: BUILDING LOVE, JOY, AND COMMITMENT
COURSE NUMBER: CG-0655

Social Security Number (USA ONLY-optional)			Personal CGSP Number*			Date of Birth (MONTH, DAY, YEAR)	

Name (First, Middle, Last)		Home Phone

Address (Street, Route, or P.O. Box)	City, State, or Province	Zip/Postal Code

CHURCH INFORMATION

Church Name

Address (Street, Route, or P.O. Box)	City, State, or Province	Zip/Postal Code

CHANGE REQUEST ONLY

☐ Former Name

☐ Former Address	City, State, or Province	Zip/Postal Code

☐ Former Church	City, State, or Province	Zip/Postal Code

Signature of Pastor, Conference Leader, or Other Church Leader	Date

*New participants are requested but not required. Thereafter, only one ID# is required. **Mail to:** C...

...ng SS# for the first time.
(615)251-5067.

Rev. 10-01